The Ancient Tithe

The Ancient Path to Happiness,

Wisdom and Financial Abundance

Dane Marks

Copyright © 2020 Dane Marks Academy

First Printing 2020

ISBN: 9798707033094
Imprint: Independently published

Table of Contents

Introduction 1

Chapter 1 3

God Always has a Plan................................... 3

The Tithe is Holy 6

Chapter 2 10

Eight Truths About the Tithe........................... 10

1.   Give of the First Fruits   14

2. Tithe Where His Title Abides........................ 15

3. Tithing Is Worship.................................. 16

4. Give Offerings Beyond the Tithe 17

5. Get the Tithe Out! 19

6. Don't Eat Your Seed!............................... 20

7. Tithes Aren't Best for Unclean Use 21

8. Your Tithes Aren't for the Dead 22

Chapter 3 25

The Benefits of Tithing 25

Devourer Rebuked for Our Sakes! 26

Your Hard Labor Will Bear Fruit...................... 27

Your Own Investments Will Prosper.................... 27

Chapter 4 29

Naked Before God 29

The Order of Melchizedek 32

Chapter 5 47

Will a Man Rob God? 47

Will a man rob God? ... (Malachi 3:8) 49

Gross or Net? 55

The Accursed Thing 58

Hidden Among their Stuff 64

Chapter 6 81

Tithing and Giving in the New Treatment 81

The Devourer Rebuked 81

Tithing the Tithe 87

CHAPTER 7 98

Why Spiritual People, Places and Organizations Should Tithe?
.... 98

Our Finances Belong to God 98

We place our confidence in Him. 98

Invite God in to Our Giving and Finances 109

Blesses Those Who Give to You 115

Allows Greater Spiritual Help, Wisdom and Inspiration Throughout Other Spiritual Places 119

CHAPTER 8 124

Why Businesses Should Tithe? 124

Allow Yourself and Your Business to Partner with God 127

Detach Yourself from Attachment with Money Knowing God Will Always Provide 130

Deeper Financial Wisdom and Greater Financial Decision Making . 136

Focus On Serving Your Customers and Staff, Trust God To Make All Else Good 140

Considerations: 145

Accrual accounting basis 145

Examples Of Businesses Who Tithe 146

CHAPTER 9 148

Why Governments Should Tithe? 148

Enriches The Economy 151

Help Spiritual People, Places and Organizations Do More Good 155

CHAPTER 10 162

Why We Should Teach Tithing People to Practice? 162

Tithing Is a Personal Experience 162

Acquire more money 162

Send facts 163

Offer skills. 163

Smile at people. 163

Attaining Consistency 164

Teach People to Reflect On Their Experience with Tithing 165

What are our attitudes? 165

1. Start Small 167

3. When you earn taxes, please determine how much money you are returning. 168

4. Practice Consistency 168

Economies of Government Officials That Tithe 169

Auto Biography

I thank you Lord most high for your wisdom and blessings.

It is my intention for this book to inspire the faithful to tithe to their local community people and places of spiritual help, support and inspiration, and to expand Gods kingdom both within and without.

O' Blessings to all the faithful who spread the positive spiritual words and kindness of God to the nation. My Name is Dane Marks and I am a servant of the Lord. It was my intention to establish such a book as this for many years, it is only now I am blessed to do so from mine and others experience of this powerful ancient principle.

I hope in my heart this will become a benefit to many local spiritual people, places and organization, to start the faithful on the path to true abundance.

I hope that people will use this book in the heart it is meant, to ensure there local spiritual centre, has what it needs to grow and share the blessings of God and continue to expand his kingdom.

I believe that those suffering from lack, will read and take the principles of this book into there hearts and that the lord will bless them and give them the true wisdom of his intervention into their financial world.

I am blessed and thankful to all who helped in the creation of this book, even before it was written.

Love, Truth and Divine Blessings. Rev. Dane Marks

<u>Introduction</u>

God is interested in every facet of your own life --such as your finances. In reality, Jesus Christ had a whole lot to say about finances and money, and the way we, as the faithful, must run our financial issues. Many Christian individuals have stated, "Money is the root of evil" and, consequently, these folks virtually have a vow of poverty and produce everyone else to endure that perception against becoming prosperous and blessed in material reality. The bible doesn't state that money is the root of evil! Let us find out what it will say...

For the love of money is a root of all kinds of evil, for which some have strayed from the faith in their greediness and pierced themselves through with many sorrows. (1 Timothy 6:10)

It's the love of cash that's the origin of evil. Cash is neither excellent nor poor; it's the way it's used, which makes it so. Money has a grip on numerous people's minds and lives. I've found that you don't need to get any money whatsoever for this to have a grip on your life as money is through all and in all. Generally, this type of money energy is in the lifestyles of people who just have a small amount! Poverty is a curse. God wants you to be blessed. However, he would like to emphasize for one reason, and that means that you can subsequently be abundant. In the last several decades, some people have advocated wealth for wealth's sake. I feel that in these past days, we'll observe a fantastic abundance hauled from the church. Not so the faithful may party, but so that the wise words of the Gospel can be soulfully preached into the hearts and minds of the community!

I will make you a great nation; I will bless you and make your name great; And you shall be a blessing. (Genesis 12:2)

This was God talking to Abraham. It's stated that Abraham became wealthy! (Gen 13:2). The motive that God blessed Abraham was he, in turn, became a King! If you're loyal to comply with God's Word together with the small amount you currently have, God will provide you more. Why should God give you £1000 if you aren't faithful using the £10 you do have?

You are going to learn a principle within this novel that will allow your finance to be utilized powerfully. Employing this principle, you can attain fantastic things in this realm --and God will permit you to be mightily blessed. Within this book, you'll see the principle of God's realm, which will release financing into your own life --financing that will supply and protect you and that you could do great with! This principle is tithing. It's the financial tool that can see you flourish from the realm of God and permit you to be a blessing to all those around you. It's but one of those necessary things that of the faithful ought to be aware of and practice within their walk with God. I know the Holy Spirit will show you this crucial kingdom reality as you examine the Word of God in this region.

Chapter 1

God Always has a Plan

For the earth is the Lord's and the fullness thereof. (1 Corinthians 10:26).

We're owners of nothing whatsoever, however, predicted to be faithful stewards of all that God blesses us all with. **For we brought nothing into this world, and it is certain we can carry nothing out. (1 Timothy 6:7).**

To put it differently, everything about the surface of the earth belongs to God. There's absolutely nothing we introduced into the world, and there's similarly nothing we could take when we depart. As straightforward as this is to grasp in regard to many things, the faithful have traditionally been incapable or reluctant to take this notion in regard to that which they consider as their cash. The accuracy of the situation is, God has blessed you with everything for your growth and requires only that you return the tithe or even ten percentages of your growth. To tithe is to go back to God, ten percent of everything he's given for you. Inherent in our openness to tithe is your recognition of God's ownership of all on and within the ground, such as our finances. Hence, the tithe must be a reflection of your admiration and thanksgiving to God for what He's done in your lifetime. It shouldn't be viewed as a weight or even a reduction; however, it should be viewed as the opportunity that it is that you flourish in the matters of God.

And all the tithe of the land, whether of the seed of the land or of the fruit of the tree, is the LORD'S: it is holy unto the LORD.

And if a man will at all redeem aught of his tithes, he shall add thereto the fifth part thereof.

And concerning the tithe of the herd, or of the flock, even of whatsoever passeth under the rod, the tenth shall be holy unto the LORD.

He shall not search whether it be good or bad, neither shall he change it: and if he changes it at all, then both it and the change thereof shall be holy; it shall not be redeemed.

These are the commandments, which the LORD commanded Moses for the children of Israel in mount Sinai. (Leviticus 27:30-34)

Notice from the very first verse we are advised that the tithe belongs to the Lord. It isn't mine or yours to do with anything we choose since it doesn't belong to people, it goes to God. In

Proverbs 3:9, we're taught to "Honor the LORD with thy substance, and with all the first fruits of all, thine increase" The material of our financing is that which we must honor the Lord, thanking Him for its supply to fulfill our requirement on earth. The first fruits are equivalent to this tithe. So any place in the Bible it describes first fruits, you understand that additionally goes to the Lord. But if you are a fantastic businessman, you understand the tithe of your company goes to God. Just ninety percent of your company is yours, and the first fruits of your gain ought to be exhibited as tithes in respect of the Lord. As the faithful, the other ninety percent of the time is yours with God. The rest ought to be invested in time of affirmative prayer, providing service, and communion with God. Similarly, your own body is your temple of the Holy Spirit, on loan to you from God. It had been bought with a price tag, and also on the day of reflection, you'll need to provide an account of the way you completed faithful obligations. What I want you to see Young of God, is that tithings are blessings. It's not something that's been set up for a vote for us to choose whether it is the perfect thing to do if we wish to expand Gods kingdom. God claims the first fruit, the first ten percentages of your growth as His. It's committed and put aside for His follower's security and expansion. Individuals produce a variety of reasons as to why they shouldn't, couldn't, or wouldn't tithe.

They say things like, "Well, it is an Old Testament matter, and because it is not said in the New Testament, we do not need to tithe." Other folks attempt to warrant not tithing by stating that "God certainly isn't transferred by something as essential as money." The dilemma is that up till today, many have not known God's heart with this topic, and in so doing, have missed out on the blessings we are assumed to during tithing. Working through scripture, we'll demonstrate that tithing is a brand-new mandate, covenant problem, and a chance to invite God into our finances. Victory in your life is decided by the way you manage the tithe.

The Tithe is Holy

As we found in the previous chapter, the tithe is sacred. It goes to the Lord, and it's sacred. Getting sacred has nothing to do with the way you dress or live. It is not in external things. Holiness is the condition of being one with God. It is the condition of being of one mind with God. It is being one with divine intelligence.

To be holy is to learn what the ancient scriptures imply, and also to be following what God request to establish his people and kingdom. From the Old Testament, there was something else considered sacred and sacred unto God, which has been the Ark of the Covenant. This sacred, mobile torso; combined with both associated things, the winner chair and cherubim; has been the significant, sacred thing to the Israelites through the wilderness period. Also known as the Ark of the Lord, this was the only article of furniture at the private area or Holiest of Holies of' Moses' tabernacle and of Solomon's temple.

It is something particular, which an individual couldn't only touch it irreverently. It was holy that if you touched on it accidentally, you'd perish. From the Bible, the term "departure" is interpreted because of separation. And when a man reaches the tithe, or mishandles the tithe, parting from God happens. When you are sacred, all of the Ancient Scriptures says is wrong is what you say isn't right. No matter what the Ancient Scriptures says is correct is everything you say will be right. When the Bible claims that acting in a specific manner is sin, well, that is what you state is sin. That is holiness. When he states that the tithe is sacred, and we know the significance of holiness, we then start to observe the tithe as something which keeps us in agreement with everything God has guaranteed and for good reason.

God has provided a covenant, and then he has given us this method known as tithing, which will be an avenue where we keep or violate the arrangement. To tithe is to keep up the arrangement between you and God, to help establish his kingdom and to support his faithful. God is good, when tithing we are expanding his good.

On the contrary, not to tithe would be to split arrangement with God. Tithing the tithe is the procedure where you introduce your tenth to Jesus, our High Priest : both the Author and Finisher of our faith. Whenever you're tithing the tithe, you're continuously confirming your arrangement together with God, and together with all the covenant guarantees connected to this tithe.

The difficulty most folks have with Leviticus 27, is it's from the Old Testament. Because It's located in that part of the Bible, many folks will say that they do not need to get that as a commandment from God and think that we're regulated exclusively by the New Testament. Well, oh faithful, this is precisely what I understand relating to this, Ancient Scripture

Dilemma. If we're not required to maintain the total Bible, then God could have given us just the New Testament. You might have been led to feel that because some publishers print those tiny green Bibles that just incorporate the novels in Matthew to Revelation. We do live under the New Testament; however, the Old Testament is still a foreshadow along with a base. It acts as a pillar to retain great knowledge and affirms that the position of the New Testament. But how bound are you? Is this only an Old Testament dilemma? Would you dismiss the commandments about tithing since you think yourself a New Testament Christian? Well, now, let us back up a tiny bit. Let us go into the book of Genesis and reply to this query.

Let's determine once and for all if that is an Old Testament dilemma or if it's a covenant problem. The next chapter of Genesis starts the saga of a guy by the name of Adam. He had been, as you might be aware, the very first person we see at the restructuring of the planet. I didn't state that he had been the first person on the ground, but that is a discussion for a different book, yet another moment. God is speaking to Adam. He offers him everything in the Garden of Eden, ability, and also all these other fantastic items and makes claims of what's to come.

Then in Genesis 2:16-17, He says, **"...Of every tree of the garden thou mayest freely eat: But of the tree of the knowledge of good and evil, thou shalt not eat of it: for in the day that thou eatest thereof thou shalt surely die."**

Well he can just eat ninety percent of the Garden of Eden. God expressly told Adam not to eat from this committed tree. God was telling Adam that they'd have the ability to keep up the arrangement they had, as long since Adam didn't touch that which was God's, is this to understand the foundation of where the tithe came from? The achievement of the arrangement was predicated upon whether Adam touched the committed thing. So far as God was concerned, if this occurred, the arrangement was away and that he would need to different from Adam. You are probably saying, "He'd eat of this tree, and also the Bible says that he will die, but he lived a few hundred years." There was a departure, a separation that happened in that circumstance. The attractiveness that Adam was walking, the guarantee to walk just like God, and be just like God was finished. He touched on the knowledge of good and evil. And, because he touched on it, the arrangement became different --to not be reinstated until somebody came to redeem the offense.

Chapter 2

Eight Truths About the Tithe

From the subsequent article, we locate a few interesting things to note about tithing. It had been given to the people throughout the Time of this Legislation. But we must bear in mind that the tithe is a Universal Kingdom principle rather than regarding the law or some other age or dispensation.

And it will be, if you come in the land that the LORD your God is giving you as an inheritance, and you possess it and live in it,

You will take some of this first of all of the produce of the earth, which you will bring out of the land that the LORD your God is giving you, and set it in a basket and then go to the location where the LORD your God chooses to make His name abide.

And you will go to the Person Who is a priest these days, and say, 'I declare today to the LORD your God I Have come to the state That the LORD swore to our fathers to provide.'

Then the priest will take the basket from your hands and place it down before the altar of the LORD your God...

'And today, behold, I have brought the first fruits of the land that you, O LORD, have given me' Then you will set it before the LORD your God, and worship before the LORD your God.

That means you shall rejoice in every fantastic thing which the LORD your God has given for you along with your residence, both you and the Levite and the stranger who's one of you.

When you have finished laying aside All of the tithe of your increase from the next season; the entire year of tithing; also have given it to the Levite, the stranger, the fatherless, and the widow, so that they may eat within your gates and be stuffed,

Then you will say before the LORD your God: 'I have removed the sacred tithe from my residence, and have given them to the Levite, the stranger, the fatherless, and the widow, according to your entire

Commandments which You have commanded me I have not transgressed Your commandments, nor have I abandoned them.

'I haven't eaten some of it once in mourning, nor have I removed any of it to get the unclean use, nor given it to the deceased. I've obeyed the voice of the LORD my God, and have done according to all that You have commanded me.

Look down from Your holy habitation, from heaven, and bless Your people Israel and the land That You have given us just as You swore to our fathers, "a land flowing with milk and also honey.; Deuteronomy 26:1-4,10-15

To start with, let us know where he is talking to those of Israel about entering the promised land and, even once they entered into the promised land, they were planning to provide the very first fruit of their property to God. Now, just as scholars, do we have to wait patiently to enter the promised land? No, we're in the promised land, and we all entered it that the instant we had been born! Consequently, the very same principles apply, since the children of Israel went in and possessed the land, once we have our salvation; thus, we encounter this kind of connection with God. From there on, we ought to present our tithes to Him.

Many of the faithful are under the misconception that we'll possess the blessings of God in "the sweet by and by." Folks have stated, "When we reach heaven, that is where the blessings will be thrown out... Then we'll have cash, " there is no point on preventing our blessings here and now in providing our first fruits to the lords kingdom on earth.

So Jesus answered and said, "Assuredly, I say to you, there is no one who has left house or brothers or sisters or father or mother or wife or children or lands, for My sake and the gospel's,

"Who shall not receive a hundredfold now in this time; houses and brothers and sisters and mothers and children and lands, with persecutions; and in the age to come, eternal life.

Mark 10:29-30

Jesus informs us that we'll receive lands and houses (material wealth). NOW within this moment! The only thing we'll want and need at the era to come is eternal life!

1. Give of the First Fruits

"...you shall take some of the first of all the produce of the ground..." Deut 26:2

Some of the faithful have stated, "God took our past £10!" He did not! God wants us to tithe the first fruits. You need to tithe FIRST! If faithful would comprehend the ability of tithing, it might be the very first thing which they do!

For if the first fruit is holy, the lump is also holy; and if the root is holy, so are the branches. Romans 11:16

As you tithe about your finance on Gods people and places from your hand, it gets the rest of your finances blessed!! Perhaps you have been compensated on a Thursday, and from Tuesday, all of your covers have gone? For the horror, you find you may not even recall what happened to it! You may see soon that the Ancient Scriptures includes a guarantee in Malachi 3, which deals with this specific issue.

The rationale that your money slipped through your hands is that you aren't tithing FIRST! All you have to do would be to take your coverslip or pay packet and different the tithe initially. Place it aside. Our spiritual centre, like most spiritual centres, supplies an envelope, particularly for this objective. Pray the prayer in the rear of the book over that quantity, and after that, the very first chance that you have, place the tithe from the church.

2. Tithe Where Gods Name Abides

...Put it (the tithe) in a basket and go to the place where the Lord chooses to make His name abide." Deut 26:2

"Bring all the tithes into the storehouse, that there may be food in My house..." Malachi 3:10

The tithe belongs to your neighborhood spiritual centre, that is the storehouse. However, not just any spiritual centre. The tithe goes into the area where God chooses to make His name abide!

"For where two or three are gathered together in My name, I am there in the midst of them." Matthew 18:20

When a church assembles at the Name of Jesus, then Jesus' presence will probably be manifest in this location! If Jesus finds himself at a meeting, then there's POWER in this location. Healings occur, the unsaved are stored, and miracles happen! A church that has God's stamp of approval to the tithes is one that's alive to the things of God. If nothing happens on your church and you're a member of "the very first church of the selected suspended," then enter a church in which his title abides! A lot of men and women state, "our church is great, there was a time back in 1956 we saw a movement of God..." Notice the Scripture stated where He left his title ABIDE... not a formal abode or a past calendar year, but where people are becoming born again and are alive with Gods blessings, love, joy and abundance... Perpetual existence of the ability of Jesus Christ! That's the type of storehouse or church wherever your tithe should go.

3. Tithing Is Worship

"...Then you shall set it before the LORD your God, and worship before the LORD your God." Deuteronomy 26:10

We see here the attraction of this tithe is the act of worship to the Lord. We are blessed if we are to worship Him with everything that we've got. As we worship him having a tenth of our growth, scripturally, we're worshipping him with our growth! Everything that you need belongs to God anyway... He's gracious, and He allows us to maintain 90 percent of it!

"And you shall go to the one who is priest in those days..." Deut. 26:3

Who's our high priest now? The Lord Jesus Christ. When we place our tithes and our offerings to the basket because it moves about, then we're introducing our offerings to the Lord. As we worship God together with our tithes, we will be mightily blessed. Tithing, such as most of the domain principles, relies on our mindset. If you merely pay the tithe from religious duty or compulsion, that is not the best path of Tithing, it is best to do it in the knowledge of supporting Gods kingdom on earth, to help the faithful help and inspire others. Tithing is now worship. We worship God with all our tithe. We tithe as we love God and desire to please Him. We Tithe because we like to love God and to invite Him into our soul and life experiences.

But lay up for yourselves treasures in heaven, where neither moth nor rust destroys and where thieves do not break in and steal.

For where your treasure is, there your heart will be also. Matthew 6:19-21

4. Give Offerings Beyond the Tithe

When you have finished laying aside all the tithe of your increase in the third year, the year of tithing, and have given

**it to the Levite, the stranger, the fatherless, and the widow..."
Deut. 26:12**

Every third season, as stated by the reference books, I've observed they had a year-old particular tithing, where they paid a tithe in their tithes. Assuming you gave £1,200 annually for three decades. It could add around £3,600 during that moment. In this year, you'd provide an additional £360, a tithe in your tithe, into the Levite (the five-star ministry), the stranger, the fatherless, and the widow. If we return into the method by which in which the temple has been set up, we notice that the priests at the ministry were taken care of; they obtained the fund to perform their job. Here, then, is an additional offering over and above the tithe that you can give in to the Levite, the stranger, the fatherless, and the widow. An offering to these people! Here is the only mention I find from the Word of God for its tithe used to provide to anybody other than into the home of the Lord, aside from the people directly involved with the ministry.

However, it's crucial to be aware it is a tithe of the tithe... It's isn't itself. Your tithes are to go to your storehouse, not to bless a visiting ministry or purchase books and tapes with. They're all for its storehouse, the neighborhood church. We do not observe any additional reference to utilizing the tithe for another purpose in this way, and surely there's not any reference to it from the New Testament. If you paid a tithe above your tithe nowadays, we'd likely call it a love offering. The Ancient Scriptures teaches it is crucial to offer offerings and above the tithe weekly. You ought to care for people who minister to you personally, and people in need. Bless your warrior! Bless the visiting ministry! Bless the widow!

5. Get the Tithe Out!

"Then you shall say before the LORD your God: I have removed the holy tithe from my house..." Deut. 26:13

If your tithe is cash, it's best to separate the tithe once possible and put it in a different envelope. Subsequently, cover that tithe at the next church meeting! Do not own it hanging around your home... Get the tithe outside and enable the blessings to enter in the remembrance of giving the first fruits, this is where the power is. Occasionally people go on vacation and, all of the time they're away, their spiritual centre receives no tithe from these.

Is this robbing God and robbing yourself from your blessings? As we'll find in the following chapter, we could bring a curse upon our own life if we don't tithe! If you're an employee, your business will cover you as you're on vacation every year. Thus, have you ever been raised throughout this time? –if YES! We will need to keep in mind we tithe if we grow. That's the principle.

How lucky we are when the faithful say, "Pastor, we're likely to be off for three months, but here's our tithe for these three months" These people today understand they are interested in being blessed while they are gone! Frequently they'll place three cheques in 3 individual envelopes and indicate each one to get another week. These faithful will be blessed because their mindset is one of dedication to the kingdom and also needing to remain connected financially with the Father's wisdom and blessings.

6. Don't Eat Your Seed!

"...I have not eaten any of it when in mourning..." Deut. 26:14

Among the worst things which you can do is to consume your seed. So many faithful overlook God's prosperity only because they refuse to run the straightforward fundamentals of God's Kingdom. If you tithe, you allow God to bless you! Whenever you don't tithe, God can't bless you. It isn't that he doesn't wish to bless you, He does, however, you've ceased that benefit from being discharged in your life via your own disallowance.

If you are willing and obedient, you shall eat the good of the land; Isaiah 1:19

Some individuals say, "We could not afford to tithe this week we needed to purchase different things..." Would you understand what you are doing? You are disallowing your seed to be blessed! I understand single mums in my spiritual organisations that are so loyal to tithe weekly. Then other men and women say, "Dane, when I do not tithe. I'll run out of cash by the end of the week. However, should I tithe I've got cash leftover," They inform me they don't understand how it works--however, it will! It's a kingdom guideline! The whole universe operates on what you give, you will receive. It's the very principle God used to establish all herein.

Imagine you're a man with ten acres to plant, and you wanted ten kilos of seed to sow this, and you also said, "Let us eat half this. We are going to grind down this stuff and intake ourselves the same bread" How much could your area finally create? **As you sow, so shall you reap.** If you consume from the tithe, you're robbing God, his kingdom and you're robbing yourself.

7. Tithes Aren't Best for Unclean Use

"...nor have I removed any of it for an unclean use..." Deut 26:14

Unclean use (unblessed use)... Indeed, that has to be hiring films with my tithe or purchasing a lottery ticket using it. Maybe gaming with it.. Unblessed usage is any use not given from the Words of God. Meaning that in case you purchase your little woman, a pair of sneakers onto it...It's an unblessed use of the tithe. If you purchase books and tapes using the tithe...Its unblessed. Should you use it to cover your consultancy charges....unblessed use. Your tithe may simply be used for a single item, to be awarded to Gods Person, Place or Organization where you receive your spiritual help and inspiration. There are tens of thousands of the faithful who don't walk into the blessings of God since they refuse to comply with the simple knowing of Gods Kingdom! If we'd do things, the right way, we'd be blessed, and Gods kingdom could do more good!

8. Your Tithes Aren't for the Dead

"... nor given any of it for the dead...." Deut. 26:14

Do not set your tithe into lifeless works. Before we attained a complete understanding of God's Word in this region, we sowed a seed to lifeless places in which the gospel wasn't being preached. We felt sorry for them and believed our fiscal present would help. It probably did assist them! However, it did very little. It had been sowing to a lifeless work. After you do so, you won't understand the fruit of your tithing and giving. You won't notice it multiply since it is sown to a lifeless work. It's not superior dirt to float into, tithing to need of the first fruits, will attract need into your life, its better to teach those in need to tithe. I've said it before, and I shall say it, find a place where the Word of God is more wealthy and robust, where the faithful are becoming born again each week, in which the Word of God is dwelling in the hearts of these individuals, where households are being constructed, and the faithful are becoming edified.

That is the place you sow your tithe! If you have been a farmer, do you simply throw your seed everywhere? If you just take your seed and then haul it all over the area, so then a few of it would go in the dam, a few on the street, and a few on your neighbor's property! The outcome would not be any harvest! We have to put our hearts in to being good stewards within the fund that God puts to our hands. Merely giving the first fruits to some job as you feel sorry for this isn't good enough! "But, if I do not remain in the Spiritual organisation and then provide my tithes subsequently, the job will shut down..." Then allow the item to shut down! When it is God, then it is going to stay whether you're there or not! Some people remain with a sinking boat, hoping to make a huge difference. They also sometimes remain in a church in which nothing occurs and in which the one thing that grows is your ivy on the walls! Their hearts could be appropriate before God; however, through that time, they need to ask God to show them what needs to be done and to show them the way forward!

You're accountable before God, because he is the constant source of who we are to be at a Spiritual Centre that feeds you and frees up you to perform the works of his will, which is doing our part in keeping his faithful and kingdom fruitful! A malevolent predator prepares the soil, waters that the harvest, and reaps the crop. Your harvest will arrive should you float in an ideal way, in the ideal location. If we'd be regulated to God's word in the region of tithing, not only could the church have been mightily blessed along with the kingdom complex, but we'd also observe the monetary blessings released to our own lives. In my years as a spiritual leader in enriching peoples lives and minds, I can be sure of something, and tithing is a kingdom theory that operates. It works for me; it functions for all those in my spiritual movement, and it works for any of the faithful from the realm of God that will dare to become hospitable to knowing the ancient secret inner knowledge and wisdom of tithing!

I have obeyed the voice of the LORD my God, and have done according to all that You have commanded me." Deut 26:14

Chapter 3

The Benefits of Tithing

In the Word of God, we could realize there are many advantages and reasons to tithe. I've stated before that God never expects you to put money into his kingdom without even planning to get a return on your investment. We've realized this to be authentic with faithful and salvation with tithing.

"Will a man rob God? Yet you have robbed Me! But you say, 'In what way have we robbed You?' In tithes and offerings".

"You are cursed with a curse, for you have robbed Me, Even this whole nation."

"Bring all the tithes into the storehouse, that there may be food in My house, and try Me now in this," says the LORD of hosts, If I will not open for you the windows of heaven and pour out for you such blessing That there will not be room enough to receive it."

And I will rebuke the devourer for your sakes, so that he will not destroy the fruit of your ground, Nor shall the vine fail to

bear fruit for you in the field," says the LORD of hosts; Malachi 3:8-12

The state of Israel, and a lot of the spiritual organisations now, were in a place of lack since they didn't tithe. We will need to see that when we do not pay our tithes and provide many offerings to God, we're robbing God, and ourselves as extensions of God. The tithe belongs to God. Until, in our reality we have paid over and above the tithe, we haven't given! The tenth component of all our growth continues to God's Kingdom.

Devourer Rebuked for Our Sakes!

"And I will rebuke the devourer for your sakes..." Malachi 3:11

Here is the only time in which God informs us that he can rebuke the wrongdoers on us. Underneath the New Testament, it's all up to us to maintain the wrongdoers beneath our feet. We do so by walking at the success God has given us through Jesus Christ. Since you tithe, God Himself rebukes that the devourer on us! We all will need to do is declare his defeat within our financing and walk from the prosperous place God has given us! Dedicated to doing right for his kingdom.

Your Hard Labor Will Bear Fruit

**"...So that he will not destroy the fruit of your ground..."
Malachi 3:11**

When the wrongdoer may, he'd ruin the fruit into your lifetime. He'd like to bring to nothing that the job of the hands-on, however, if you're a tither that he can't do it! You will flourish in your work area. The job of your hands will bring about much benefit, and you'll be blessed!

Your Own Investments Will Prosper

"... neither shall your vine cast her fruit before the time in the field..." Malachi 3:11

Your vine in your area is investment. It's the cash you have working for you. That fund won't cast its fruit before its time! A guy in our spiritual organisation offered his organization and neglected to tithe about the growth he'd had in his company. He had learned the other prosperity principles but failed to understand Tithing element and supportive role to us, who helped him achieve his success through our spiritual principles.

He spent that money on everything other than us. You know he came to me weeks after telling me he had been losing thousands of pounds each month within his business and other money was slow in coming, and also there wasn't something that he can do about it? But there is, he could tithe and bring the power of God to bless his finances into his life.

The cash was locked out for ages! I advised him to regret not tithing and begin to tithe to his growth from this time. Within weeks his finance turned about and started to generate income! As a tither, you can guarantee your spirit-led investments into God's Kingdom will flourish you! Your homes will consistently bring at the ideal lease; your shares will merely increase! Your company is only going to grow more reliable and more powerful! God will guide you how to make the best investments and if they don't work at any point in time, he will bring the blessings to you. You cannot out give God.

a promise between at least two parties to perform the conditions agreed upon. A covenant could only be broken from death when it's created in blood. We do not have to produce arrangements of this kind now because we now have the blood of Jesus, but back then, that is the most potent kind of arrangement known to man. All through in the next section, we see God creating and affirming His claims to Abram, whose title has been changed to Abraham.

And I will make thy seed as the dust of the earth: so that if a man can number the dust of the earth, then shall thy seed also be numbered. (Genesis 13:16)

And there came one that had escaped, and told Abram the Hebrew... And when Abram heard that his brother was taken captive, he armed his trained servants, born in his own house, three hundred and eighteen, and pursued them until Done.

And he brought back all the goods, and also brought again his brother Lot, and his goods, and the women also, and the people. (Genesis 14:13,14,16)

Abram was in conflict, won the struggle, and got the spoils of this conflict. Pay careful attention to precisely what Abram does with his growth.

And Melchizedek king of Salem brought forth bread and wine: and he was the priest of the highest God.

And he blessed him, and said, Blessed be Abram of the highest God, possessor of heaven and earth:

And blessed be the highest God, which hath delivered thine enemies into thy hand. And he gave him tithes of all. (Genesis 14:18-20)

Look what is occurring O Faithful of God, directly in the center of the covenant being put, we find this guy bringing from the tithe. Now, allow me to put this on your soul: Wherever you locate a tither, you are likely to locate success. Wherever you discover a non-tither, you are likely to locate the failure. The covenant promises of God may always be made for somebody who will keep remaining hooked up into this covenant through his tithes.

And the king of Sodom said unto Abram, give me the persons, and take the goods to thyself.

And Abram said to the king of Sodom, I have lifted up mine hand unto the LORD, the highest God, the possessor of heaven and earth.

That I will not take from a thread even to a shoe latchet, and that I will not take anything that is thine, lest thou shouldest say, I have made Abram rich... (Genesis 14:21-23)

What is he saying? "I do not need anything out of you. I'm likely to continue to tithe. I will present my first fruits to God, and nobody will have the ability to say that they left me wealthy, but God Himself." In the subsequent chapter, they are getting prepared for the covenant service. Abram wished to understand how he'd inherit all of the things God promised him. Before this in Genesis 15 the Bible informs about the respective creatures required for the service, and also the procedure for cutting the faithful covenant.

"In the same day, the LORD made a covenant with Abram, saying, unto thy seed have I given this land..." (Genesis 15:18)

And I will make thee exceeding fruitful, and I will make nations of thee, and kings shall come out of thee.

And I will establish my covenant between me and thee and thy seed after thee in their generations for an everlasting covenant, to be a God unto thee, and to thy seed after thee. (Genesis 17:6-7)

God changed Abram's name to Abraham when the covenant was cut between these. If tithing is part of the covenant-making procedure between God and Abraham, along with the Ancient Scriptures, states that this is an everlasting covenant, then who is contained in the covenant? According to the scripture, you simply read, you are.

In Galatians 3:29, the Bible says, "If ye be Christ's, then are ye Abraham's seed, and heirs according to the promise."

That simply means that what God promised Abraham. He also promises for you. Throughout this interaction with the High Priest, He promised Abraham that he'd bless him. Abraham brought the tithe to the High Priest and in doing so he had been blessed. Acquiring the tithe was the route in which Abraham can partake in the covenant promises of God. This is what the majority of people from the Body of Christ incline to perform. We sing tunes about Abraham's blessings, but we seem to overlook how he obtained the blessings. You notice, you cannot receive the guarantee if you don't receive it via the procedure displayed in Genesis 14:18 as it states, "blessed by Abram of the highest God"--an affirmation of that which he promised to perform sooner. It's by way of this tithe that God managed to perform his promise of blessings to Abraham. Because Abraham represents all people if we do what he did afterward, we will get what God promises in our own lives, precisely the identical manner Abraham obtained them to function in his lifetime.

Everyone, these guarantees put together to include the Abrahamic Covenant. Because the Bible claims that this covenant is endless, there's not any limit to the guarantees made or into the blessings guaranteed. Bearing that in mind, does this finish in 1998? Can you finish in the calendar year 2000? Can it finish after we have been raptured? No, because of the ceaseless way without ending. Consequently, if tithing a part of the Abrahamic Covenant, does this make a difference which you just read about it from the Old Testament? It does not. It is a part of an everlasting covenant that communicates, and that breaks the bounds of their New Testament. For all those who believe we modern-day Faithful need simply to reside by the Spiritual Centre, I say this: We're covenant people. We do our part for God and the kingdom.

Not only might we live by the Spiritual Kingdom, but we're also all heirs of the Abrahamic Covenant, and whatever from the Old Testament that is still part of the promise God made to Abraham, and is pertinent and good to our own lives now! Therefore, anyone who tells you that tithing isn't suitable for now, which was only for the older covenant saints is confused and just by the act of testing the tithe in your own life, you would see the absolute truth of the power of God in your own experience. You will need to swiftly take them throughout the Word of God and reveal that tithing is part of an unending, eternal covenant when it comes to people today and it is a truly blessed and good way of life when we bring God's Kingdom into our finances. And, God takes us if we need Abraham's promises in our own lives now, to precisely the identical way Abraham honored him. Follow me? Considering all the scriptures I have provided you, and I know in my soul that a few of you're still battling the concept of committing to God, ten percent of everything to go to his kingdom on a regular and disciplined basis. But truly I am not here to convince you, but I have the working knowledge of this principle so will share this with you. It is the love or fear and attachment to money that holds most of the faithful back.

The Bible states in the book of Timothy, the love of money is the root of evil. However, do you understand what that says if it speaks about the worth of cash? It is truly about getting the incorrect connection with the material universe. Inside of you at the moment, in case you've got a funny feeling this Welsh Spiritual Teacher is attempting to talk you into just giving ten percent of your cash to your local church, then you are under the effect of not having the benefit of testing God in this. I cannot make it any plainer than that which you've read. You cannot accuse me of giving you my interpretation and I don't really care if you do, as I work for God in this matter, for the purpose of his kingdom, but I simply led you throughout the Ancient Scriptures.

Turn to Luke 11:42. Notice that it's Jesus talking here. You can tell because it's written in red.

"But woe unto you, Pharisees! for ye tithe mint and rue and all manner of herbs, and pass over judgment and the love of God: these ought ye to have done, and not to leave the other undone."

They are tithing every one of these various things. He explained, "You tithe, and you need to." Jesus Himself is telling them they should tithe but added when they tithe, they're not to omit the weightier things, like the love of God and ruling. You cannot behave like a fool and tithe. There are different things you should consider.

You've got to be loyal and to trust God when you become a tither, his wisdom and blessings will fill your mind and experiences. Jesus says you need to tithe. If you are wondering why I have not yet taken one to Malachi, just be patient. We'll arrive at Malachi in a Moment. You might not wish to go to Malachi after what you are going to see. You might never wish to browse Malachi again so long as you reside. You might even be more likely to rip that book from your Ancient Scripture once you read what is coming up.

So also Christ glorified not himself to be made a high priest; but he that said unto him, Thou art my Son, today have I begotten thee. As he saith also in another place, Thou art a

priest forever after the order of Melchisedec. (Hebrews 5:5-6)

Was not this Melchisedec, the exact same high-profile Priest of the God most high that Abraham, brought his tithes to? This scripture is saying Jesus is a High Priest forever, after the order of Melchisedec. Precisely what's he saying? This Jesus is a High Priest, which he'll function in precisely the same way Melchisedec functioned in. That means if we would like to learn about Jesus' priesthood along with Just how it is to function, all we must do is figure out just how Melchisedec's priesthood worked. That which we understand is that Melchisedec obtained the tithe!

Who in the days of his flesh, when he had offered up prayers and supplications with loud crying and tears unto him that was able to save him from death, and was heard in that he feared;

Though he were a Son, yet learned his obedience by the things which he suffered;

And being made perfect, he became the author of eternal salvation unto all them that obey him;

It does not seem so from the New Testament. But if you are unaware of precisely what the order of Melchisedec is, then you won't understand what the word tithing does when looking at Jesus as a descendant of the order of Melchisedec, it has to be read in the Ancient Scriptures. For many years those who can't rightly understand the word are telling you it does not get seen past Malachi, it does, but does that matter really anyway? Talking of Malachi, let us go there. This is where it will get somewhat private. Now, would you think that tithing is the will of God? After studying this novel, how a lot of you say you are likely to do this for the remainder of your everyday life? Only God knows for sure.

A number of you are probably saying you will not ever read some of the books because I took up each of those pages to discuss the tithe. You are likely complaining you don't have sufficient money today to pay your accounts, and here I'm speaking about returning ten percent of everything you get. Believe it or not, tithing isn't a money problem, its a money benefit and blessing, but you need to take the actions to activate its blessings in your life. If you'd like the things of God, like financing to cover your accounts, you need to trust His Word and the process of tithing in your experience. This is the way you go about shifting from being a non-tither into a tither. To start with, you end up in an atmosphere in which the Word is moving forth and God's wisdom in tithing becomes obvious. Visit your spiritual organisation and enter an atmosphere in which you feel God's presence. Tithe your tithe of your first fruits. The only way that you alter is to acquire the Word with understanding. In the event you do not feel the positive Word that is going on, you have not gotten it on your heart, ask god to guide you where to put your tithe. Whenever I think of a sermon, your becoming relies on whether you knew it and embrace it. There are loads of preachers preaching sermons people are not getting, is this the word you want to help expand? Is this truly the Kingdom of God? continue to ask God to guide you where you should be getting your spiritual support, help or inspiration, and trust his guidance.

Chapter 5

Will a Man Rob God?

Malachi 3:3

And he shall sit as a refiner and purifier of silver: and he shall purify the sons of Levi, and purge them as gold and silver, that they may offer unto the LORD an offering in righteousness.

Righteousness is a word. At any time, you hear someone speak of the right-standing using their faith in God, understand they are talking about covenant. What this means and is saying is that they might provide just a single offering in line with this covenant. Realize that this O Faithful of God, to provide an offer, is to produce an offer. Simply because you create an offer, does not follow that the deal was committed too. I can provide you £100 to your vehicle, and it is worth £5,000. Simply because I make an offer for you does not signify you need to take it.

Similarly, with God. What should you consider on Sunday mornings once you twist plunk your own £2.50? What do you say if I told you that perhaps, just perhaps, this was not a commitment as it was below the tithe and not committed on a regular and disciplined basis? What we will need to understand as the faithful would be when an offering is approved, and once it's rejected, since I mentioned before, not all of the offerings are obtained.

Which is the reason for which you have to see the reflection of the full tithe and above in your own experience. Here you're walking around believing you have seed from the floor, and maybe God did not take you up on your deal. You are thinking that you are giving God a museum that offers, and He is saying, "No, you cannot provide Me because it is not provided based on covenant. It is not being provided at righteousness."

Then shall the offering of Judah and Jerusalem be pleasant unto the LORD, as in the days of old, as in former years.

And I will come near to you to judgment; and I will be a swift witness against the sorcerers... (Malachi 3:4-5)

...And against the adulterers, and against false swearers, and against those that oppress the hireling in his wages, and the widow, and the fatherless, and that turn aside the stranger from his right, and fear not me, saith the LORD of hosts. (Malachi 3:5)

For I am the LORD, I change not; therefore, ye sons of Jacob are not consumed.

Even from the days of your fathers ye are gone away from mine ordinances, and have not kept them. Return unto me.

And I will return unto you. Saith the LORD of hosts. But ye said, wherein shall we return? (Malachi 3:5b-7)

He is speaking back to Abraham when He discusses those days of the fathers. The term "ordinance" means sequence. At this time, you cannot help but inquire here, "What sequence is He referring to?" When he says reunite, you cannot return something that was not there at the first location. When he states "return," that's an unambiguous presentation of market, and that is what covenant is all about. There is always a market in the covenant. There is a market of weaknesses for strengths. He stated, "You return to Me, and I will go back to you" To put it differently, there are several things that need to be traded here. Some things which are no more being traded due to something which hasn't yet been returned.

Will a man rob God? ... (Malachi 3:8)

The answer to that question. Can a man rob God? The solution is an emphatic, yes! Have you robbed God? He is speaking about what He is getting prepared to describe as an intruder. There's such a thing as God-robbing, which in turn is robbing ourselves. And, precisely what you need to ask yourself is this: Can and have I, as the faithful, robbed god?

Yet ye have robbed me. But ye say, wherein have we robbed thee? In tithes and offerings. (Malachi 3:8b)

You might have been providing an offer, but the deal you made wasn't given based on covenant. An offering to the kingdom of God will need to be done on a regular and disciplined basis and at the ten percent required. Directly speaking, you cannot offer a valid offering before you give to a representative of the Kingdom of God, who is establishing Gods kingdom on earth. And, as you're attempting to place seed in a stone floor to acquire symptom, God states, "I do not get it since it is not presented based on righteousness, and it is not fine to Me."

Allow me to put this differently. My team blessed me having more people to my seminars through a current academy members appreciation. Say, for example, I offer you my people to attend your congregation, you maintain them consistently and provide me £10 per week to get gasoline. I don't need £10 out of you. I would like my new members back. Give me my members back again. But every week, you return to me together with all the £10, and that I refuse the cash. It is the Exact Same way with God. Every week that you are and offer Him a couple of bucks, and it is not the tenth as requested. He does not need to have the offering until you've shown to be loyal to the tithe. His word is, as you're not providing the tithe, He cannot provide you with full deliverance, peace, or prosperity. He is not giving you whatever His Word says that you could have, as you are still holding on to a thing that belongs to theirs. Everything stops till you give God back what's rightfully His. Afterward, He is able to return multiple blessings to you.

Do not become mad and place the book down. God has given a means out to you! It might be that your blessings are locked in

Heaven since His substance is locked in your bank accounts. I understand this might come as a harsh saying to you personally; however, you cannot expect that random offers are obtained by God if you are not even a tither. That is only a pure, simple fact. Regardless of what you have been told by your spiritual organization and the proof will demonstrate itself in your own experience. Now see:

Ye are cursed with a curse: for ye have robbed me, even this whole nation. (Malachi 3:9)

If you should contact some Hebrew Bible, you'd observe this previous scripture states, "I offer you a final note of this cancellation of the arrangement." It's as if an insurance provider sends you a notice of cancellation because you never paid off your premiums. If you are in a crash, they are not obliged to return and bless you as you kept what was theirs, as stated by the contract you've signed.

Thus, God is putting you on sight. Every single time you continue to not offer this tithe; He is sending you a note in the email your contract is going to be terminated.

Bring ye all the tithes into the storehouse, that there may be meat in mine house, and prove me now herewith, saith the LORD of hosts, if I will not open you the windows of heaven,

and pour you out a blessing, that there shall not be room enough to receive it. (Malachi 3:10)

I have discovered the storehouse is a person of God; however, that I take issue with this statement. I think since it's employed here, Jesus is your storehouse. A storehouse is a location where all of the spiritual tools and the teachings are derived and taught. The distribution of everything comes from God into the church and is then spread. As a person of God, I cannot afford anything unless it is given to me from God. I am in the supply center. The storehouse is the person who has the spiritual distribution and will function as a provider of spiritual help, support and inspiration. I am only able to disperse that which comes in my palms. Distributor standing comes after you have shown yourself at the stewardship section. Many men and women believe an individual is mechanically a steward only because they sow seeds to the realm.

"Moreover it is required in stewards, that a man be found faithful." (1 Corinthians 4:2)

God won't select you to be a steward, won't cause you to be a supply center, until you are found loyal over this with which he's entrusted you. You have to pass the test of faithfulness. He won't give you what is your own till you've

shown yourself loyal over what is just another man's. (Luke 16:12)

God directs the distribution as well as your leader, in turn, may provide the blessings to you and your blessings to the faithful. So long as the Word of God is moving forth in the pulpit of the spiritual organisation, that is where your requirements are being fulfilled.

The Word of God is your needful thing. Just as you turn to the T.V. and somebody excited you and induced chill bumps to show up in your arms, that is not a sign to send cash designated to your regional church, or around the nation, although you will still be blessed, it is better to support your local place of worship to benefit those local to you. If he's not the person who feeds the Word into you always. Suppose that the application is faulty, then what exactly? Unless God informs you to tithe into a television ministry, then your sowing ought to be performed in house land. Simply because you enjoy what you watch on T.V., that isn't a sign that is where your tithes should be routed as our focus should be on our local spiritual place. But if you are not getting fed on the regional church, then you will need to pray and ask God for direction regarding where you ought to be attending.

For all those who attend megachurches and also have an issue with being unable to shake the warrior's hand, then remember this: The warrior didn't die on the cross for you, Jesus did. Consequently, you do not come to meet some guy, and you are to listen to the Word of God. I have even heard some people today say that since they pay their tithes, they have the right to meet with the warrior. Should you read the ancient scriptures, you'd understand that Moses was rebuked with his father-in-law for trying to govern a lot of people?

A phrase from God came for him to appoint advisers within the public and split them into groups. We use this program in our spiritual organisation, and it functions nicely. The only counseling I do will be by the pulpit. When my buddies come to attend my spiritual teachings, they receive the answers they require in my sermons. If this does not do the job, I've got a catalog of tapes on just about the broadest assortment of spiritual topics out there. Get on the mind; you don't pay tithes to meet up the warrior. It is not an entry ticket, and it is tribute and thanksgiving to God. You do not pay tithes into the warrior. The tithes do not belong to the preacher; the tithe belongs to God, to help establish his kingdom and help those in it. You do not pay tithes to acquire a private audience with your warrior, and then you cover them to be blessed by God. Do not make the mistake of producing your warrior as your origin, as he is human in service to Gods kingdom.

Make God your origin, the highest universal expression of love. Should you invest the quality time at the Word, and also spend time going to your spiritual organisation, and spend time in the Holy Spirit communicating with God, in an authentic fashion, you will not have to have anyone counsel you but God Himself. God is making you an offer you can't refuse. Bring the tithe and observe Me on the windows of Heaven. Bring the tithe and find out what I could do with you. After A spiritual organisation I know started with eight associates, each of these were tithers. The ability of God was all around the area. After the spiritual organisations started to grow, symptoms diminished. I asked the Lord why he explained:

"What happened was that before, you had one hundred percent tithers, and the windows were opened one hundred percent. Then the crooks started coming in. Those who wanted the Word, but didn't want to tithe. God-robbers started joining the church. They hooked up with you and affected the whole nation, and the windows closed down to eighty percent."

At that stage, we just needed eighty percent tithers, meaning eighty percent symptom. It's gone steadily down as the number of individuals joining the spiritual organisation has significantly improved. The manifestation we desire will be held up due to their thieves, the individuals who'd dare to commemorate God. If we want to bless our lives and the lives of others, tithe and teach them to tithe and reflect from their own experience, create a powerful community around you of tithers and openly speak of the blessings god has brought to you, see the power of the kingdom we will establish and the things we will accomplish.

Gross or Net?

The Faithful will always ask when they are supposed to tithe off the gross income, or away from the net income of the paychecks. Tithes are obtained from the growth, and what exactly you're raised by is your gross profit. The net only seems since the government does not trust you enough to ship them their ten percent so that they take it outside until you receive it. If you bought a vehicle for £3,000, then turned around and sold it for £3,000, would you tithe of this? No. Why? Since there wasn't any boost in that circumstance. On the flip side, if you bought an automobile for £3,000 subsequently marketed it for £3,500, you're accountable for repaying the extra £500 increase.

You'd tithe £50 out of this trade. When there's a rise, there is a tithe. Should you chance to borrow cash, there is no need to tithe since there's not any increase. You have only incurred a debt that has to be paid back. At this time, you've set yourself in the situation of being a faithful servant to the person who gives you the cash. (Proverbs 22:7)

Additionally, when you get an income tax refund, then it isn't vital to tithe on this because the authorities are refunding the above and over they obtained from you during the year. That is money you ought to have been tithing on altogether, so there is no requirement to tithe on it. The tithe is your covenant connector. It links you to the covenant promises of God. Regardless of what you tithe, covenant law states that is what you may have in return. Should you sow time, then you are going to receive time.

If you sow service, then you're going to receive support, and should you sow cash, you're going to receive cash. God can offer a crop out of the tithe in these kind of ways, an increase, a financial gift, incentive, or another sort of financial growth. The tithe is what will hook you up into the numerous promises of God. As God told Abraham in the Old Church to establish His covenant, he's telling you how to do precisely the same thing, O Faithful of God. When you set his covenant in motion to being committed to the tithe, God will lead to manifestations to happen in your experiences. At any time, you touch with the tithe off the first of your fruits, you also touch with the covenant.

At any time, you respect the tithe, and you honor it, you are bringing God into your finances and you will be blessed in many ways. Many say to me, in the many years that I have been born, I have never known the seriousness and power of tithing before today. I never connected the tithe as what linked me to the claims of God until today. I recognize like never before this when recovery is guaranteed for you in his Word, not tithing will interfere covenant of recovery from coming into your entire financial experience. If you see in the Word in which God has assured you security, subsequently tithing will ensure you receive that coverage you had been guaranteed. Do not allow your incorrect connection with the content world to block you from getting what is yours. You hear a sermon on tithing, and also, the very first thing happens is that you become fearful that the preacher is attempting to acquire your cash. This is because the spiritual organization isn't teaching correctly the power of the tithe from the perspective and experiences of the tither and the blessing the tither receives with their financial connection with God.

The panic comes in along with the incorrect belief that you are in a situation in which the claims of God cannot come to pass on your and in your current and future experiences. The negative aspects of our mind, does not care one way or the other regarding the cash because most people spend their money on things they really have no real need for anyway; however, I do care about you becoming in alignment with what God has promised you and expanding his good on earth. So that you can avoid the dread, that the Word of God won't come in your own life where the advantages of tithing are involved, so you can tithe and experience the blessings of god for helping his faithful and word spread forth. Then you will avoid this fear that a self-fulfilling prophecy since as you aren't tithing the Word of God can't function to provide the blessings God has guaranteed.

The Accursed Thing

How severe can God take this matter of tithing? I have experienced that God with all His love, and all His mercy and kindness couldn't let me endure when I failed to bring the ten percent to his storehouse, before I studied and taught this ancient principle. Within this part, I'll show you just what God knows about people who transgress His Word about the tithe and who are worried. Come with me into this book of Joshua, the initial thing, and we are going to start this feature of the conversation with all the walls of Jericho. As a kid attending Sunday school, all I knew was someone walked around that wall seven days. It was only a recent revelation that come to comprehend that tithing is part of the narrative.

Within this circumstance of scripture, they consult with the tithe because of the "committed" or even "accursed" thing. The term "accursed" means dedicated or committed, so once you read that speaks concerning the accursed thing, it's speaking about the tithe. In those days they called the tithe, the accursed thing, as to take something which belonged to Gods Kingdom could deliver a curse. It had been accursed since it represented what could happen to you when you made the mistake of touching God's stuff. Notice what's happening in those verses in Joshua, also to where the temptations are.

(Joshua 6:1-16)

Now Jericho was straightly shut up because of the children of Israel: none went out, and none came in.

And the LORD said unto Joshua, See, I have given unto thine hand Jericho, and the king thereof, and the mighty men of valour.

And ye shall compass the city, all ye men of war, and go round about the city once. Thus shalt thou do this for six days.

And seven priests shall bear before the ark seven trumpets of rams' horns: and the seventh day ye shall compass the city seven times, and the priests shall blow with the trumpets.

And it shall come to pass, that when they make a long blast with the ram's horn, and when ye hear the sound of the trumpet, all the people shall shout with a great shout; and the wall of the city shall fall down flat, and the people shall ascend up every man straight before him.

And Joshua the son of Nun called the priests, and said unto them, Take up the ark of the covenant, and let seven priests bear seven rams' horns before the ark of the LORD.

And he said unto the people, Pass on, and compass the city, and him that is armed pass on before the ark of the LORD.

And it came to pass, when Joshua had spoken unto the people, that the seven priests bearing the seven trumpets of rams' horns passed on before the LORD, and blew with the trumpets: and the ark of the covenant of the LORD followed them.

And the armed men went before the priests that blew with the trumpets, and the rearward came after the ark, the priests going on, and blowing with the trumpets.

And Joshua had commanded the people saying, Ye shall not shout, nor make any noise with your voice, neither shall any word proceed out of your mouth, until the day I bid you shout; then shall ye shout. So the ark of the LORD compassed the city, going about it once: and they came into the camp, and lodged in the camp.

And Joshua rose early in the morning, and the priests took up the ark of the LORD.

And seven priests bearing seven trumpets of rams' horns before the ark of the LORD went on continually, and blew with the trumpets: and the armed men went before them; but the rearward came after the ark of the LORD, the priests going on, and blowing with the trumpets.

And the second day they compassed the city once, and returned into the camp: so did they for six days.

And it came to pass on the seventh day, that they rose early about the dawning of the day, and compassed the city after the same manner seven times: only on that day they compassed the city seven times.

And it came to pass at the seventh time, when the priests blew with the trumpets, Joshua said unto the people, Shout; for the LORD hath given you the city.

Thus far, everybody should know what this collection of scriptures is all about. God gave Joshua, and his people a command to walk around the city once each day for seven days, and on the seventh day to stroll around the city for seven times. The wall was made to supernaturally, fall, and Joshua and his men managed to move in and have the town. But now, see this:

And the city shall be accursed, even it, and all that are therein, to the LORD: only Rahab the harlot shall live, she and all that are with her in the house, because she hid the messengers that we sent.

And ye in any wise keep yourselves from the accursed thing, lest ye make yourselves accursed, when ye take of the accursed thing, and make the camp of Israel a curse, and trouble it.

But all the silver, and gold, and vessels of brass and iron, are consecrated unto the LORD: they shall come into the treasury of the LORD. (Joshua 6:17-19)

Because you can see, Rahab, the harlot has been permitted to live as she hid the spies Joshua had shipped in to test things out. Due to the covenant, she's being blessed since she was fortunate that she supported a man of God. And, although the guys are being told what to do to see success, they're given a warning regarding the accursed thing and advised to keep away from it. The accursed issue is that of this gold, silver, iron, and brass, plus they appeal to God. As in those verses of scripture, the tithe is giving into the treasury of the Lord. The one thing which may cause defeat for us and Joshua's individuals is that of the mishandling of God's possessions. On the flip side, we're sure to live a life that is successful, protected and blessed when we respect the Lord with all the first fruits of our growth as well as our substance.

So the people shouted when the priests blew with the trumpets: and it came to pass when the people heard the sound of the trumpet, and the people shouted with a great shout, that the wall fell down flat, so that the people went up into the city, every man straight before him, and they took the city. (Joshua 6:20)

That's the success they had achieved through the power of God, so clearly, they managed the tithe properly. Nobody touched the thing that is committed. At the approaching poetry, we see that the harlot Rahab and her dad's family being blessed as a result of her actions for Joshua.

And Joshua saved Rahab the harlot alive, and her father's household, and all that she had; and she dwelleth in Israel even unto this day; because she hid the messengers, which Joshua sent to spy out Jericho. (Joshua 6:25)

This specific guarantee came to pass for Rahab since Israel honored God using all the committed entities, and since I have attempted to reveal through scripture, this is what connects you with all the claims of God.

I will bless those that bless you and curse those that curse you. (Genesis 12:3)

It clearly shows how success can come in your life if you honor God together with all the tithe and offerings to his kingdom. On the other hand, nevertheless, let us see if you genuinely wish to keep investing God's money by mishandling the tithe. You will discover that it only could be better that you exude that trip into the mall, and then give God what is rightfully His, the blessings are to good to miss and assisting your spiritual organization and faithful is far more important.

Hidden Among their Stuff

Proceed with me now to Joshua 7:1:

But the children of Israel committed a trespass in the accursed thing...

A person sinned. Someone touched on the tithe.

...for Achan the son of Carmi, the son of Zabdi, the son of Zerah, of the tribe of Judah, took of the accursed thing...

Therefore, the promise comes by faith, so that it may be by grace and may be guaranteed to all Abraham's offspring—not only to those who are of the law but also to those who have the faith of Abraham. He is the father of us all. [17] As it is written: "I have made you a father of many nations."[c] He is our father in the sight of God, in whom he believed—the God who gives life to the dead and calls into being things that were not.. (Romans 4:16)

...and the anger of the LORD was kindled against the children of Israel. (Joshua 7:1b)

It is possible to enjoy the blessings of God if you pay your tithes to his kingdom, but when others touch on the Tithe not using it for his kingdom works, will indeed anger God. Does it upset the Lord when just a small number of this church has been bringing the tithes into the storehouse. Due to the crooks touching the accursed thing. What happens is that you've got people wondering when God is about the task since they cannot observe the energy of God working in peoples' lives. Yes, this makes Him mad. Read on:

And Joshua sent men from Jericho to Ai which is beside Bethaven, on the east side of Bethel, and spake unto them, saying, Go up and view the country.

And the men went up and viewed Ai. And they returned to Joshua, and said unto him, Let not all the people go up; but let about two or three thousand men go up and smite Ai; and make not all the people to labour thither; for they are but a few. (Joshua 7:2-3)

So there went up thither of the people about three thousand men: and they fled before the men of Ai.

And the men of Ai smote of them about thirty and six men: for they chased them from before the gate even unto Shebarim, and smote them in the going down: wherefore the hearts of the people melted, and became as water. (Joshua 7:5)

What occurred here is that, poor Israel came to conflict believing they'd easily wipe these out, men and women who shouldn't have been an issue, simply to get 36 men immediately defeated and chased back into the gate.

And Joshua fell to the earth upon his face before the ark of the LORD until the evening, he and the elders of Israel, and put dust upon their heads.

Then Joshua tore his clothes and fell facedown to the ground before the ark of the LORD, remaining there till evening. The elders of Israel did the same, and sprinkled dust on their heads. [7] And Joshua said, "Alas, Sovereign LORD, why did you ever bring this people across the Jordan to deliver us into the hands of the Amorites to destroy us? If only we had been content to stay on the other side of the Jordan! (Joshua 7:6-7)

To put it differently, "God, why did you draw us to receive our Butts being kicked? This is not what the lord does.

Pardon your servant, Lord. What can I say, now that Israel has been routed by its enemies? (Joshua 7:8)

What a cowardly action. His guys looked weak since they ran from the enemy. What exactly was he going to convey about all of the men and women that were convinced they needed to end the problems of them not being able to defeat the enemy.

And the LORD said unto Joshua, Get thee up... (Joshua 7:10)

Joshua knew that God would have not allowed his enemies to defeat him through his knowledge of the Universal heart of God, he was unaware of why this situation has happened. He reaches out to the lord for his wisdom. He calls upon the lord to show him what had happened.

Israel hath sinned... (Joshua 7:11)

Does it shock you that God would call stealing from the tithe a sin? Many of you do not even think about it as a sin as you believe it your cash. You believe you have the right to perform with all the tithe at you will, once the tithe is given, it is for the people of the spiritual centre to use it for Gods works as he guides them to do so.

...And they have also transgressed my covenant which I commanded them: for they have even taken of the accursed thing, and have also stolen, and dissembled also, and they have put it even among their own stuff. (Joshua 7:11)

Here is the image. They have sinned from the covenant. And, in so doing, God isn't able to deliver His promises to maneuver in their own lives. He guaranteed success, healing, deliverance, and prosperity, but he cannot give them these things. They did not understand the direct connection between the covenant as well as the committed thing. What about you? Have you ever taken God's tithe and set it on your stuff? Have you deposited ten percent on your bank account when it ought to have been in God's treasury, I have, before I understood this tithing, and lived the unblessed life of poverty, deprivation and failure. And if it's amongst your things, how frequently have you ever done this thing? How frequently have we mingled the items with God's items? The trend the majority of us have would be to justify mimicking the tithe by stating,

"I worked and earned this money" However, and the Bible has made it rather apparent. The tithe of the earth is the Lord's. What you do not appear to realize is that if it weren't for God, there would be no ground, no atmosphere, no one --so He needs to be the first for each of the tithes of the planet. Consider it. Without God, you would not be here, and you'd not be a human being if it not for Him. The Lord is only wanting us to look after his Kingdom, and anyone who dares to attempt and justify not giving to God's Kingdom and to connect their finances to him to be blessed, Inform me of this, to your Job, can you shape yourself? How do you breathe with no oxygen God provides? The utility business will switch your lights off if you do not pay them. However, God remains to let the sunlight shine on the just and the unjust. Do not tell me He isn't a merciful God. If He were not, he'd cut off your oxygen each time you did not produce the tithe. Do not tell me He isn't loving and kind, all knowing and all loving. It is only that we honor the covenant. God continues to do

His role, but we must do our part too. God is constant and will never violate His covenant. It includes blessings and curses. Not through God, but through our detachment from the deeper wisdom in dealing with tithes and offerings.

Therefore, the children of Israel could not stand before their enemies, but turned their backs before their enemies, because they were accursed: neither will I be with you anymore, except ye destroy the accursed from among you. (Joshua 7:12)

For many of those that are non-tithers, I wonder just how hard a time you are having standing against the opponents. Can you stand against illness or disorder? Can you stand against the stresses of the world and so that you do not cave in, give up, stop, and backslide? Under normal circumstances, you can deal with these items, but something out of the ordinary, currently becomes an ordeal, how frequently does this happen to you. All because we got God's things mixed up along with our stuff.

One thing must be understood with the process of tithing the first of what we receive, is that this simple act is the act of allowing our supernatural connection with God, it is the connection that allows the ability of Gods Kingdom to get established, maintained and furthered, it is not for the free picking of anyone not administering for Gods kingdom purposes.

It says in 1 John 1:9, "If we confess our sins, he is faithful and just to forgive us our sins, and to cleanse us from all unrighteousness.

We now have the option of visiting God's Kingdom and speaking to Him for the forgiveness of our sins, that is what Jesus provided. The children of Israel did not have an identical option. God informed them point-blank, "I will have nothing to do with you till you destroy the accursed from among you." It has been their sole option. He explained when they locate the man or woman who touched the dedicated thing and ruin him. Until then He wasn't likely to get anything else.

The tithe is the powerful connection between us and God, it opens and maintains a gateway between us. I wonder what could happen if God were to do this now? Cannot you see just how much we are operating under the power? Suppose God were to say, "All right, do not tithe, see if I care, I stopped. I am not likely to get anything to do with you till you fix it" Lots of people are living lives in which you have not fixed those occasions when they have not tithed to God since, each time you believed to do the ideal thing, as you felt like you were not able to tithe since you could not see the way you were planning to make it till the end of the month. The irony of this is that if you began doing what He demands of you, He would have the ability to show you a few things you could not see and bring things that were not previously there. The very reason why they cannot see before the conclusion of the month will be since they have not committed to Tithing, and His divine intellect is cut away from them. The children of Israel have only one way from the scenario:

Up, sanctify the people, and say, Sanctify yourselves against tomorrow: for thus saith the LORD God of Israel, There is an accursed thing in the midst of thee, O Israel: thou canst not stand before thine enemies, until ye take away the accursed thing from among you. (Joshua 7:13)

You've got enemies, people! The devil is the adversary. He wants you dead, so weak, blinded, and confused. Even the Bible says if you are not tithing, you cannot stand against your enemies. Satan isn't your buddy. He'll not be your buddy. He needs you pitiful and in Hell on earth. He wishes to be in a position to laugh at you even if all is finished and done with as you are in Hell on earth with him.

So Joshua rose early in the morning, and brought Israel by their tribes; and the tribe of Judah was taken: (Joshua 7:16)

And he brought his household man by man; and Achan, the son of Carmi, the son of Zabdi, the son of Zerah, of the tribe of Judah, was taken.

And Joshua said unto Achan, My son, give, I pray thee, glory to the LORD God of Israel, and make confession unto him; and tell me now what thou hast done; hide it not from me.

And Achan answered Joshua, and said, Indeed, I have sinned against the LORD God of Israel, and thus and thus have I done: (Joshua 7:18-20)

Even Achan understood he'd sinned, but we've got people that struck the tithe and behaved as though they haven't done something wrong. As though their job to devote all that comes in their hands.

When I saw among the spoils a goodly Babylonish garment, and two hundred shekels of silver, and a wedge of gold of fifty shekels of weight, then I coveted them, and took them; and, behold, they are hid in the earth in the midst of my tent, and the silver under it. (Joshua 7:21)

That is what a few people can perform. You find the amount of money it is possible to keep on your own. You realize that you're donating money to the spiritual organisation you could've used to pay your light bill or purchased a new dress or a suit. If you desire something, you wish to own from someone else and have something that's not yours. That is what God was talking to Moses about if He cautioned him to not covet something which has been his neighbors. If you covet what you do not own release it. You attempt to have hold of something which does not necessarily belong to you personally. In this case, if Achan gets the material hidden at his property.

If I had to ask you now where God's substance was, you would probably say it is at the bank, or under your bed, or even concealed in your shoe. I don't know about you, but I am motivated by what I see within the blessed wisdom of the scriptures. You want to realize is that in one stage in my entire life, I did not believe in tithing. I felt like I'd worked too difficult to acquire the little cash I had, simply to have a preacher stand and inform me I needed to give up ten percent. It has been one of these "no calculate" scenarios for me before I awakened. And I am not speaking about waking up in the religious sense. I mean, I woke up one afternoon and after watching Rev. Edwene Gains and realized that I had missed out the tithing principle in my prosperity teachings and experience. The very first thing that I asked was, God, teach me about this principle of tithing, so I would teach others, and this started my path of tithing and truly living blessed.

God, why did this happen?" And He said, "The devourer came in, just like he was supposed to." All of a sudden, I got the revelation of the scripture that promises He will rebuke the devourer for my sake. (Malachi 3:11)

Guess what happened when I turned into a tither? I didn't need to have the devourer carrying anything out of me. When that comes to pass, the cash you are attempting to continue to will leave anyway, as you have got to substitute something which has been lost, broken, or stolen. One way or another, you are likely to reduce it. What goes around comes around, and in case you are stealing what belongs to God, somebody or something will steal everything belongs to you personally. Lord have mercy. The truth about this statement is, pay attention to where your first fruits are going to, if your not tithing, they are usually going to some form of bill or debt. Wherever the first of your money goes, increases the essence of that in your life. Give to the universal creator and sustainer of all things and you will be able to create and sustain anything you choose and destroy the ill will or intent of anyone who stands against you. Your life will become blessed and all things you do becomes under the protection of the Lord most high.

So Joshua sent messengers and they ran unto the tent; and behold, it was hid in his tent, and the silver under it.

And they took them out of the midst of the tent, and brought them unto Joshua, and unto all the children of Israel, and laid them out before the LORD. (Joshua 7:22-23)

Now I had been believing, praise the Lord, it is around, but it was not over whatsoever. Bear in mind, and God had told them he wouldn't be back till they ruined the particular person who'd touched on the tithe. That is what God said. Let us just imagine what it'd be like now if God hadn't given us the grace and pity we are currently beneath. We would most likely have a personal computer system that you may need to get until you arrived at the church. To be able to enter, you'd add a card that will lift the entrance gate. If you weren't a tither, then you'd be detained in the reception, then brought down to endure ahead of the church. Even the ushers would then hand out stones and guns to everybody.

After all of the transgressors were lifeless, God could return to our area of worship, also then we might have church. On the program, each Sunday is the time set aside for choosing out each one the crooks and eliminating these so God can come in the area. We do not understand how blessed we will be under this contemporary system. This guy's sin affected his whole family. They were being judged since the mind of their family transgressed the covenant. Allow me to tell you something, guys. Do not rely on your wife to get the tithe, and you make sure the tithe has got in. That is your job for a person of God and also the mind of your loved ones. Your loved ones can be lucky or cursed, dependent on the way that the family is managing the tithe. I am telling you that this powerful agreement is quite serious.

In times when I have stopped tithing or put something before the Kingdom, I have found that the blessings of my life have become less and that I cannot achieve the strong success I have wanted. In one company where I had been tithing faithfully, the control of the money went to another and the company ended up completely failing.

Here we had been awaiting our return, and God was awaiting His also. Therefore, while we had been still waiting, the devourer came and did devouring. The moment I realized in what we'd failed in, we started to tithe again straight away. An affirmation of the significance of sowing the seed arrived months later after, when I had established my spiritual academy and taught tithing and prosperity principles, now my academy members thrive, unmoved by external circumstances why others react to external material circumstances trying to control these matters to establish their businesses and institutions. Now, return to Achan. It might be a little difficult for many of you to take; however, Achan's brothers, sisters, as well as the family pet were going to endure for something Achan failed.

And Joshua, and all Israel with him, took Achan the son of Zerah, and the silver, and the garment, and the wedge of gold, and his sons, and his daughters, and his oxen, and his asses, and his sheep, and his tent, and all that he had: and they brought them unto the valley of Achor.

And Joshua said, why hast thou troubled us? the LORD shall trouble thee this day. And all Israel stoned him with stones, and burned them with fire, after they had stoned them with stones.

And they raised over him a great heap of stones unto this day. So the LORD turned from the fierceness of his anger. Wherefore the name of that place was called, The valley of Achor, unto this day. (Joshua 7:24-26)

It probably sounds barbaric and cruel to a few of you; however, that is precisely what was demanded in these days when somebody left with what happened to God. Notice the Lord turned out of his rage just as soon as they eliminate this person who had touched on the accursed thing.

And the LORD said unto Joshua, Fear not, neither be thou dismayed: take all the people of war with thee, and arise, go up to Ai: see, I have given into thy hand the king of Ai, and his people, and his city, and his land: (Joshua 8:1)

And the LORD said unto Joshua, stretch out the spear that is in thy hand toward Ai; for I will give it into thine hand.

And Joshua stretched out the spear that he had in his hand toward the city. (Joshua 8:18) And Joshua burnt Ai, and made it a heap forever, even a desolation unto this day. (Joshua 8:28)

The moment the tithe scenario was straightened out, everything fell into place. Failure and defeat, success, and achievement are based on the way someone shows that ten percent of the growth. It needs to be evident to you that you can be connected or disconnected in the claims of God according to the way you manage the cash. Additionally, you wonder if this is a severe matter.

The New Testament says, in Luke 16:11, "If therefore ye have not been faithful in the unrighteous mammon, who will commit to your trust the true riches?

No servant can serve two masters: for either he will hate the one, and love the other; or else he will hold to the one, and despise the other. Ye cannot serve God and mammon. " (Luke 6:13)

It obviously isn't only an Old Testament dilemma; however, as we discussed previously, it's a matter of this covenant between you and God. If people begin to argue with you about the requirement to tithe, do not go there together. Only offer them a copy of this publication. Allow them to see it if you must. Anything in their mind could be revived about this topic as once we feel the effects of the tithe, the tithe itself calls us into alignment with it. Do not turn the topic of tithing to a discussion in which arguments will prevail, as the tithe is an experience between God and the tither, it is a personal matter and people must be allowed to look into their own reflective experience with it. If people decide to dismiss biblical instruction after it has been brought to their attention, there is not anything you can do here, just have faith God will show them the way in his own time.

However, much cash you plant, if you are not a tither, you are likely to discover that hook-up at some phase. You first must reach the ten percentage before it's possible to supply the eleven percentage, and that's the point where the offering begins.

Chapter 6

Tithing and Giving in the New Treatment

The Devourer Rebuked

Let's return into this book of Malachi for an instant, in which God concerns that which He will do up to the devourer is concerned.

Bring ye all the tithes into the storehouse, that there may be meat in mine house, and prove me now herewith, saith the LORD of hosts, if I will not open you the windows of heaven, and pour you out a blessing, that there shall not be room enough to receive it.

And I will rebuke the devourer for your sakes... (Malachi 3:10-11a)

That term "rebuke" signifies cease, no longer! If you are being devoured, deliver the tithe and exhibit it unto God. He states He will create the prevention so others cease taking away from you. You've got the right to go to God and state, **"Lord, I deliver this tithe at this time in the middle of all of the Hell that I am in, and that I stand in Your Word. I provide you this tithe. You said in Your Word you will rebuke the devourer for your own**

interest. I anticipate this scenario that is for me to put you first from now on. I know that it's my fault and ask for your forgiveness from this point. I know I brought this on my own but Lord, allow it to quit now in the name of Jesus."

If you are getting tired of dropping each job that you get, deliver the tithe. If your vehicle was repossessed, or you have been evicted from your house, make the tithe. Bring it, and God can prevent and stop all those endangering you.

...And he shall not destroy the fruits of your ground; neither shall your vine cast her fruit before the time in the field, saith the LORD of hosts. (Malachi 3:11b)

Maybe you've been working and not able to acquire certain things to occur in your own life, and they are naturally not occurring. Whenever you don't tithe, the devourer has every right to destroy the fruits of the floor. You might even have fruit development, but it does not last long. You can earn lots of cash, but still, be unable to tell where it is moving. If my partner and I had been beginning a household, I decided my tithes were awarded consistently.

I wasn't going to possess the enemy trigger so that my spiritual academy members would lose the benefit of my tithe, the name of Jesus. We needed to create all our spiritual academy members to flourish abundantly and consistently as we flourish consistently and abundantly. God won't allow the blessed faithful to fail. Reflect on this moving forward, If your are starting a family, are you and your spouse tithing? Second, check to find out whether there's strife in your family, and thirdly, take a look at any biological problems which might be causing one to miscarry. It is possible to take your tithe and sow that tithe and state, **"In the name of Jesus, I have a right to the fruit of the body. I rebuke whatever is happening here, and at the name of Jesus, I line my entire life using all the Word of God. I thank you, God, my baby is full-term and healthy."**

Invite the Holy Spirit to that setting and then thank God ahead of conception happening. There were individuals from the Bible who did not have kids before the onset of God showed up. Think about the Shunammite woman where Elisha came? She was waiting to get a baby for quite a while; also, Gehazi told Elisha she had been bare.

And he said, about this season, according to the time of life, thou shalt embrace a son. And she said, Nay, my lord, thou man of God, do not lie unto thine handmaid.

And the woman conceived, and bare a son at that season that Elisha had said unto her, according to the time of life. (2 Kings 4:16-17)

Well, like Elisha, I am not lying when I inform you the anointing can do what you have been attempting to have done all these years. The anointing will eliminate that load of childlessness if you don't quit, cave, and stop on God. Each time you tithe, you Want to place God into remembrance by stating, **"Lord, this is my tithe. This is my covenant connector, and I bring it before You right now, and I thank You for conception and for my child. Be it unto me, according to Your Word.**

If you are walking into doubt, consider Mary. She had been advised she was likely to become pregnant, and she'd never known a guy from the biblical belief. Together with the anointing of God, all things are possible.

And all nations shall call you blessed: for ye shall be a delightsome land, saith the LORD of hosts.

Your words have been stout against me, saith the LORD, Yet ye say, What have we spoken so much against thee? (Malachi 3:12-13)

The Tithing power is extended with your words, so be sure to not use phrases to prevent the manifestations of the things you want, use your words with wisdom and into the direction of the things you want, not the things you dont. Speak under the claims of God. Do not disconnect yourself in the covenant by talking words that can prevent those blessings in these paths. Words can discontinue what the tithe has released. Words have power.

Ye have said, It is vain to serve God: and what profit is it that we have kept his ordinance, and that we have walked mournfully before the LORD of hosts? (Malachi 3:14)

Here is a good illustration of what you state that will prevent your tithe from making a crop for you: "Here I'm tithing, and that I visit this property dealer driving a much better car than mine." This type of lack awareness extended by your words, is the absence of faith. Your words can misalign your attention away from what the tithe is attracting for you. "Oh well, I don't know. I am bringing my tithe to the church, riding in an old, beat-up Toyota, along with the preacher, who is riding in a Rolls Royce.". If your preacher chooses to ride in a Rolls, then you have to thank God he is, since that is your proof that you also can get it too. Do not allow your mouth and thoughts to block you from reaping the pleasures that your tithe will bring you around. Only continue to consider the ten percent because of your covenant connector and use your words to summon the things you desire and don't condemn what you believe you don't currently have, because you will have what you desire.

Glory to God. **"Heavenly Father, I'm convinced by The Word which tithing is the way to connect our finances with you from your wisdom given to me. It's a covenant, and it's**

the will of you. Accordingly, in the name of Jesus, I won't transgress the covenant I have. Neither will I rob you of those tithes any more for the rest of my entire life. I ask you, Lord, to forgive me. I admit that if I touched on the tithe, I sinned. However, Your Word says. If I admit my sins, you're loyal. You're only to forgive me of my sins and to cleanse me from all unrighteousness. Thank You, Lord. Thank You, Lord, for your promises. I walk into them today, and I declare the top-notch connector is an enduring element of my entire life. In Jesus' name. Amen."

If you may, take some time out to worship God within the instruction and recently found knowledge you have of the topic. Proceed to Him and tell Him you encounter Him with the tithe of what that's increased in your lifetime. Ask the Lord to link you with each guarantee His Word provides to those people who adore Him. Ask to be linked to the guarantee of recovery, the assurance of deliverance, the guarantee of prosperity, and the guarantee of wealth. Request that everything He has promised in His Word has been attached to you daily. Give God the glory, the compliments, and the honor. Thank Him for controlling the devil and preventing him from devouring what is rightfully yours. Thank Him for opening doors that no man can close, and also for bringing forth prosperity in your experience. Those things you have been dreaming about and wondering why they still have not come yet, thank God that they're coming today in the name of Jesus. Do not stop to tithe, sow it as fast as it comes in your palms. No matter what you do, do not enter bondage and fear believing the warrior, the finance manager or somebody counting the cash will require your tithe and utilize it for purposes other than that which God meant it to be utilized. Your assurance is that you have completed what God have blessed of you. Woe be it unto the individual who subsequently steals what you've attracted to Jesus, your High Priest, in reverence and obedience.

As you read earlier in this publication, God has his very own unique method of managing robbers. As soon as you've sown your tithe, do not even permit with any dread your thoughts to rob one of the happiness of your spiritual giving, God knows your heart.

Tithing the Tithe

Tithing, the tithe is completed using words. God has given us particular directions about the best way to provide the tithe. It is not only assumed to be thrown into a bucket--that is called bucket-plunking. God hopes that we'll pray His Word within the first fruits by which he's blessed us before placing it in the palms of the High Priest.

That thou shalt take of the first of all the fruit of the earth, which thou shalt bring of thy land that the Lord thy God giveth thee, and shalt put it in a basket and shalt go unto the place which the LORD thy God shall choose to place his name there.

And thou shalt go unto the priest that shall be in those days, and say unto him, I profess this day unto the LORD thy God,

that I am come unto the place which the LORD sware unto our fathers for to give us.

And the priest shall take the basket out of thine hand, and set it down before the altar of the LORD thy God.

And thou shalt speak and say before the LORD thy God, A Syrian ready to perish was my father, and he went down into Egypt, and sojourned there with a few, and became there a nation, great, mighty, and populous:

And the Egyptians evil entreated us, and afflicted us, and laid upon us hard bondage:

And when we cried unto the LORD God of our fathers, the LORD heard our voice, and looked on our affliction, and our labour, and our oppression:

And the LORD brought us forth out of Egypt with a mighty hand, and with an outstretched arm, and with great terribleness, and with signs, and with wonders:

And he hath brought us into this place, and hath given us this land, even a land that floweth with milk and honey.

And now, behold, I have brought the first fruits of the land, which thou, O LORD has given me.

And thou shalt set it before the LORD thy God, and worship before the LORD thy God.

And thou shalt rejoice in every good thing which the LORD thy God hath given unto thee, and unto thine house, thou, and the Levite, and the stranger that is among you. (Deuteronomy 26:211)

These scriptures are showing us that it is crucial to go to God in prayer, reminding Freedom of those claims of recovery, salvation, peace, happiness, and all else included in the covenant you've got with Him. Picture Jesus, the High Priest, showcasing your tithe before the throne of God. At this point, you have God's focus and evidence that the arrangement remains in effect. Here is the opportunity to connect with Gods blessings in your material reality. Here is the opportunity to open your mouth and talk about those things you are thanking God for. When you complete showcasing your tithe, so it begins, creating the flow of tithing all the tithes of thine increase. Do not forget that it's Jesus you bring your tithe to, rather than the preacher. The preacher could be the one collecting the tithes; however, you've put your committed thing before the throne of God. If a person chooses to do something dumb with your tithe once you have introduced it, then that is between that person and God. You have kept God's commandment and completed everything that God demands of you. As Soon as You get it you profess:

"Lord, I deliver this tithe Before You and before the covenant of claims You've created together with my father Abraham, and together with me personally, the seed of Abraham. From the name of Jesus, I come before You placing you into remembrance of this guarantee to cure me all manner of illness, lack and disease." Jesus requires the tithe and sets it unto God and his Kingdom.

The Bible lets you continue speaking:

"I say unto You Lord; I had been a sinner in my way into Hell. I didn't have God on my side, also that I did not have Heaven in my opinion. I had been in a land of bliss being conquered on all areas, however, I recall Lord, once the physicians had given me up, the way You came and changed the report. I recall how You treated me and sent me with wonders and signs with a powerful outstretched hand. I'm to You Now Lord, thanking You Lord to the assurance of complete recovery in line with this covenant. Now, I am

linked to Your guarantee along with my tithe. I worship You Lord, also that I moan until you Lord, and I thank You Lord for all of the goodness that You are doing in my entire life. Thank You for my own occupation. Thank You I've got a place to live. Thank You I'm in a position to inhale and exhale. Thank You I've got a bed to sleep, thank you my family is very well. Thank You Lord.

Now God I announce in the name of Jesus, this guarantee You have produced in covenant relies on the tithe I have attracted to You. I have linked with all the guarantee. Jesus is my High Priest, after the order of Melchisedec. I feel that the machine put in place that states once I bring the tithe, You deliver the guarantee. Amen.

Faithful of God, because you may see, the words that you talk on your seed are extremely important. When you throw your envelope at the bucket because it moves, you are not taking advantage of the energy inherent in the Word of God. The superb thing is that God will respond with His Word, and from covenant law, he will go steps farther than your proceeds whenever you make the demonstration. Consider, for example, the situation surrounding Abraham's tithing the first fruit of the flesh, his son Isaac. Jesus wouldn't have been granted because the first fruit of revival if Isaac hadn't been given up. When God put Abraham up to provide his son as a sacrifice, He had been bound by chance to go a step further than that which He'd asked Abraham to perform.

And it came to pass after these things, that God did tempt Abraham, and said unto him, Abraham: and he said, Behold, here I am.

And he said, take now thy son, thine only son Isaac, whom thou lovest, and get thee into the land of Moriah; and offer him there for a burnt offering upon one of the mountains which I will tell thee of.

And Abraham rose up early in the morning, and saddled his ass, and took two of his young men with him, and Isaac his son, and clave the wood for the burnt offering, and rose up, and went unto the place of which God had told him.

Then on the third day Abraham lifted up his eyes, and saw the place afar off.

And Abraham said unto his young men, Abide ye here with the ass; and I and the lad will go yonder and worship, and come again to you. (Genesis 22:1-5)

Abraham didn't speak against what he'd stated in his tithing procedure. He traveled about speaking following his covenant. "Yeah, I always understand God told me to deliver my son to kill him, but I've got a guarantee with God, and I am connected. I know God will need to work out this thing since He promised my seed could outnumber the stars. Isaac might need to live so that he will create a seed so God will need to do something. Either He is going to lift him from the dead, "He has got to supply something different for me to offer you. I don't understand how this will end. However, I am in the covenant, and God will come through. I am not disconnecting till I get a reflection of what I have been sworn, so I will continue to speak based on what I am expecting. I understand the boy, and I really are coming back down this mountain!" You ought to take courses from Abraham. Rather than that, you sow your seed and then walk from their church doors, stating you cannot manage to go to dinner now, rather than announcing the prosperity and prosperity promised for you in God's Word. Otherwise, you acknowledge that you cannot envision living in that fair mansion. You simply drove past. To not worry. If you cannot envision it, you cannot get it. Anything you can picture is everything it is possible to possess.

And Abraham took the wood of the burnt offering, and laid it upon Isaac his son; and he took the fire in his hand, and a knife; and they went both of them together.

And Isaac spake unto Abraham his father, and said, My father: and he said, Here am I, my son.

And he said, Behold the fire and the wood: but where is the lamb for a burnt offering? And Abraham said, My son, God will provide himself a lamb for a burnt offering: so they went both of them together. (Genesis 22:6-8)

Why did not he simply turn into his son and state, you are precisely the offering? Since he was not moved by what he observed. He was not moved by his plight. He wasn't talking according to what was happening, and he had been talking dependent on the claims of God. Just if you feel that Abraham has been lying, think about that: The Bible says in James 3:14,"....lie not contrary to the facts." The Reality Is that the Word of God. There can be details in your own life, but these details might not lineup with the fact of the Word of God. Thus, whenever you need to select what to think, pick the Word of God, and lie not against the fact of God's Word. If the physician says you are likely to die of cancer, then the Bible claims that from the stripes Jesus endured before His crucifixion, then you're treated. (1 Peter 2:24) To select healing over just what the physician said, will alter the results of what the physician said!

Abraham and his son arrived at the location where they might hook up with that God said they might possess. There's a location at which you could figure out when you're genuine about these things you are thanking God for. It is the location where you're able to stop on God and backslide; also, it is the place you state that for God I live and also for God, I'll die. I don't know whether you've gotten there yet, but everybody is going to need to pass this test at any time in their life. As soon as you pass this test, you hear God say, "Now I know." I am entirely convinced that it is easy to become a Christian, as it is easy to become a Christian.

And they came to the place which God had told him of, and Abraham built an altar there, and laid the wood in order, and bound Isaac, his son, and laid him on the altar upon the wood.

And Abraham stretched forth his hand and took the knife to slay his son.

And the angel of the Lord called unto him out of heaven, and said, Abraham, Abraham: and he said, here am I.

And he said, Lay not thine hand upon the lad, neither do thou anything unto him: for now I know that thou fearest God, seeing thou hast not withheld thy son, thine only son from me. (Genesis 22:9-12)

Seeing that you didn't withhold the tithe, seeing you didn't withhold your seed, so I understand today. Lots of you haven't gotten into the location of "today, I understand" because it is simple for you to provide a £2.50 tithe, however, if you are raised to the stage of needing to tithe £2,000--well that is another story.

And Abraham lifted up his eyes, and looked, and behold behind him a ram caught in a thicket by his horns: and Abraham went and took the ram, and offered him up for a burnt offering in the stead of his son. (Genesis 22:13)

Rather than a lamb, God discovered his very own tithe from the ram. The ram was that the replacement, however, the guarantee showed up the same. God wanted Abraham to sow his fruit, and so that God could purge his. Abraham was prepared to sow Isaac, although he ended up needing to. The main issue is that he had been ready. That is all God had to understand. His strategy was to plant his very own Son Jesus because of the ceaseless tithe. He understood they were planning to crucify His Son, abandon Him for deceased, and He'd be buried. God knew he was going into the pit of hell, just to climb on the next moment. Jesus was climbed up the first fruit in the deceased, but if you read your Bible carefully, Jesus wasn't the only one listed to have been hammered daily.

Paradise was closed the day Jesus had been resurrected, and each one, the captive saints, came from the place since Jesus Himself was that the tithe. God Almighty is telling us how to deliver our tithes; therefore, He could do something more significant. If you feel you are giving something up, He's blessings which are exceedingly, abundantly above whatever you might ask or think about. (Ephesians 3:20) He states He will cure you deliver you better and flourish you -- all this via the tithe. He wishes to perform for you more significant than the planet's system could do to you. He is only waiting for one always to bring your tithe having a ready heart. Our prayer needs to be to request the Lord to forgive us for carrying this ten percent so gently and handling it as nothing significant. We all know, and we do. This tithing item is much more severe than we have thought previously. It is the creation throughout which God is creating a revelation so readily offered. It is info that has to be imparted to churches anywhere. Jesus is on His way back, and also we must own as many individuals victorious on the devil as you can. I feel that since we examine and are educated on this topic, God is putting us up for extreme manifestation. The established wealth God desires to bring us is intending to distribute the gospel all around the world. God provides us the prosperity to satisfy His covenant until all families of the world are blessed. (Deuteronomy 8:18)

Chapter 7

Why Spiritual People, Places and Organizations Should Tithe?

Our Finances Belong to God

Some of us say and believe that God rules it all. In particular, when things go wrong, things are hard or we seem to be in an endless trap, misery or seemingly bad luck. We speak out of faith, but often our acts are not consistent with our philosophy of belief.

For example, while we believe that God governs an aspect of life, say finance, we struggle with needs every day, like paying for the roof over our heads.

We're worried how we pay expenses at the end of the month or how we're going to endure another day. We look forward to the day when our luck turns, hopeless right now. What does our Father have to say about this?

We place our confidence in Him.

It's not our work or our lack with which we have a relationship, it's with our Family. It's not our other, partner, relative or friend with whom we connect, it's with our parent. It is not our material things, it is with our God that we have a friendship. We are not in relation to our bank account, our addictions, our loss, our hopes and dreams, but to our Lord.

We can put all trust in our Lord. Not sometimes, not when good or bad things are coming and going, but in all cases. What does this mean on a regular basis exactly?

In all things, we should work hard to ensure that before acting, that we are secured with our Lord and have invited him to work in our finances through our tithe. The first of our offerings on a regular and disciplined basis.

See it as an insurance policy. Imagine that we have purchased insurance for our products, which are safety, house, automobiles and products in the material world. We need due diligence to learn what our insurance policy covers. We ensure that when shopping in the form of products and travel, even to different places, we are protected by our insurance policies.

We buy insurance at home to cover us in case of fire, flood or robbery etc. In case something goes wrong, we hope to be protected for these issues. When we add to our homes, we make sure that we get properly insured (some insurance policy changes at this point may be enough), and if anything goes wrong, we're going to be all right.

In another case, when we plan our lives, we check in with our jobs. We check to ensure that we can go on holiday or take absence. Those are the items we test at this time, or on a regular basis, to ensure that we are protected if the needs occur.

Problems occur when we take a plunge and then assume that one of the examples is shielded. We are in trouble when we connect to the house and do not look through the insurance policies first, to find out later that we can't be refunded in the event of a flood.

If we are in a position not covered by our health / travel insurance, something will happen, we are in trouble. We cannot take time off and expect to be paid until we have completed our first homework to make sure we are paid.

We put our expectations on men, events and circumstances when things get hard. If they fall apart, we look to God, because it hasn't been working out for us. We wonder where we checked him in before we wanted to call on him for his support when times get hard.

In putting God first in all, it means finding His direction, support and safety in what we are doing and that we hope on doing. This means that our faith is first and foremost in Him. This does not circumvent the need to do our due diligence in the material world; it assumes that by doing what He asks us to do, it will all go well. It's His vow, and God isn't the one who breaks His vow.

When we first discuss with him our intention to incorporate or change our place of residence, he does more than say yes or no. It can be an economical way to do this. He will provide the best way for us to be, do and have. This is living blessed, when we can just trust everything.

God might remind us that we cannot change the position and we have to wait some time, while other issues are taken care of first. He does inform us because He knows that our condition will change quickly and when there will be no need for changes.

When we consult with HIM on our travel plans first, HE can provide valuable details for a good and relaxing trip. If we check in with HIM for time off, HE will inform us that later on the time bank will be useful when we will need to take the time off.

HE can ask us to wait, because there may be a chance to apply or qualify for it, regardless of the time period or the number of days taken off. HE will pose another opportunity while we are off, HE will teach us how to optimize the time we've taken off.

When we look for God in everything, it doesn't mean we transform into robots. It's a smart thing to do, but we're human, so we have limited sight and vision. The universal principle of All is god and it is inherent in us, it is the true part of us. God is not separate from us, we just miss the mark sometimes, his kingdom is established to remind us of who we are and put us back into alignment with ourselves, we should never see God as separate from ourselves.

When we agree, we take them with the right intentions in order to produce the best outcomes, to expect the best but to plan for the worst. God knows this in his infinite wisdom, and he sees it. HE asks us to check in with him because HE alone can guarantee this.

HE understands that we say and do things for our benefit, and HE wants to help us do it. HE needs to do so in every corner of our lives so that we lead full lives in every circumstance in which we find ourselves at the end of it.

HE gets hurts when we are overwhelmed with shattered dreams, broken expectations, relationships, families, businesses and careers. HE revels not in our suffering. HE knows how it will influence us before we do it.

When we first check in with HIM before anything, only then can HE prepare us properly for what will come. Why isn't HE going to stop it? HE knows what he made us to do, to stand and to succeed.

We also build the world in which we work together and individually. HE gave us the free will gift. God is not a man and cannot misuse His universal power and step in every step, ignoring the decisions and choices of man, regardless of the foolishness and detriment of others. But he will bless those who put him first in their life and will make miracles happen for them, it is universal law.

Freewill means someone is going to want to support someone else (choosing to benefit a friend). Free will means that someone will try to rob us (selecting this feeding route).

Freewill means that someone is going to ride in our cars (choosing or not to drive drunk). We have options in all cases, like thinking or saying we have no choice, is a choice in itself. All individual decisions affect far more than our restricted human range of perception and vision. We can never know how many lives our actions touch.

HE knows everything and sees all and asks us to check in first with him so that he can provide us with the security HIS insurance (Christ) provided us irrespective of person, issue, and circumstance. We're going to be infused with his wisdom, security and powers.

If we introduce and change our lives and expect to be protected, HE will not be able to do so if we don't affirm for his for his wisdom first. If we want to take decisions that lead us to various people, places, thoughts and acts, HE cannot shield us from problems until we affirm in pray that we require his wisdom.

If we log in and run into issues, we have the insurance plans that we have bought and the fine print which means we're protected, we can turn to HIM and say Cover Me and know we'll be safe. We're going to be covered.

When we first follow HIM in all and trust to give him the first, no matter where we go or what we do, we are assured that HE knows and sees all, and that we are so restricted in our sight and vision that we are incapable of seeing and knowing what he does, but know that HE will protect us because HE led us there. This is how people understand God to work in mysterious ways.

If we check in with HIM in all, if we don't trust people, things and circumstances HE will make us wise, HE will help us work things out. It could be that a friend asks for a loan from you. Check in first with God before depending on your friendship. If the reply is yes, lend the money.

If your friend flees from his obligation to refund you, first check in with God. He might tell you to go to your friend or ask you to let go of the situation. The Lord knows and sees what you're not knowing or seeing. In HIS time, HE will recover the money for you. At this time, The Lord will protect and teach you the heart of his wisdom as you remain blessed.

The Lord works in all our lives, all of us because we are him, and you don't know what HE wants to do in the life of your friend. What you may not see is how it will turn out at the end, but God will keep his promised to you. You will continue to be blessed regardless.

If you have ill feelings, human resentments because of your broken commitment, check in first with God. HE's going to help you. HE's going to take care of you. He will make you wise among the nations and establish your kingdom as you are establishing his kingdom for the faithful and born again.

Trust in the Lord and your covenant with him and not the person and situation as this will bring trust in yourself; God is invincible to men and to all, things and circumstances. God is. HIS promises are permanent. What you won't see right away is how HE uses all of your perspectives to work for your sakes and others.

Every big and small thing, in HIM, as with us is part of a number. The thing that created the air you breathe, the eyes you see, the Sun in the Sky, the sea. The promises that if you first check in to HIM, HE will provide all your needs (mind, body, soul) and protect them.

True infinite wealth has a spiritual base. Even as we engage with God through affirmative prayer about what we believe to be real and spiritually communicate with God through affirmative prayer, so do we offer the GIFT of Tithing faithfully in accordance with the Eternal Source of our spiritual help, support and inspiration.

"Systematic distribution opens the door to systematic reception," Dr. Ponder says. Giving God The First Ten percent of what we receive to people or places where you get your spiritual nourishment helps you to experience real wealth with wonderful results.

The ancient law of abundance is as ancient as we are a species. Tithing was the way of life of the original man who sacrificed to his gods in the ever-changing cultures of Egyptians, Babylonians, Arabs, Greeks, Romans and Chinese. "Ancients understood intuitively that the first financial step to permanent and sustainable wealth was to give. It is practiced in Hinduism called Dhama, and in Islam as Zakat. All Faiths practiced spiritual offerings. It is truly a universal principle.

Some of the twentieth century's most influential millionaires attributed their remarkable prosperity to the tithing custom. Catherine Ponder states, "John D. Rockefeller started tithing as a young man in 1855.

He made an income of $95.00 for that year and he tithed his church $9.50 from this." But she says, "between 1855 and 1934, he gave $531 million and his typical response to the critics of his generosity was 'God was giving me my wealth.'" If God is in equation, prosperity is guaranteed (meaning well-being and integrity).

So what are we doing when we give the Tithing GIFT?

We say, "Thank you, Lord," for the bounty we have got. The concept of tithe wasn't a mistake; since it has been discovered that those who tithe never know lack and limit, it has been believed that if you teach these people to do so, they will always be effective.

Tithing can occur only when people are conscious of the great gifts that God has given to them and, in gratitude, wish to share some part of it. "This sharing is just about thankfulness to God's grace, and that is why those who unexpectedly come to tithe are still kindly and abundantly cared for.

Tithing is an important aspect of gratitude that not only prospers the tither, but also the beneficiary of the tithe.

Tithing is the act of giving thanks to 100%, by leaving 10% of the person(s) or place(s) in which we recognize God's presence in life with our Source. Tithing has historically been synonymous with giving to our place of worship. "Theologians also tended to stress what the tithing would do for the church, rather than what it might do for the tither,"

However, when we investigate Tithing more closely as a spiritual activity (not a mechanical obligation), we can only infer that it is the person who will be rewarded and prospered by Tithing. The receiver will, of course, be too, because it's all about establishing and maintaining Gods Kingdom on earth.

There are numerous accounts of the economical and successful progress of the Tithing gifts as well as reflection on your experiences while you tithe.

"I have more money to spend and more clients, not less because I started and continue to tithe," says one of the students of my academy. "I placed my tithe last week, and an unexpected check that I wanted was sent out in the mail."

"From the beginning of my seminars on prosperity and my move into offering the gift of over and above the Tithe on a regular and disciplined basis of the first of what I receive, my house changed and we are more happy here. That is one of my many, many blessings, when all odds were stacked against us" I have heard that repeated: "I thrived financially and in so many different ways when I was Tithing, but after I quit Tithing and I am back to the same 'soup' I used to be in before." This is because of the incorrect teaching of tithing, where people don't have the right teacher, helping students reflect on the benefits of tithing in there own experiences.

So, what can you expect from the GIFT of Tithing when you start offering it?

1. Fear normally emerges. Now, I don't have enough. How do I ...? How can I? This gets replaced with a powerful feeling of love once you make the tithe in and around your heart. This is the birth of creation and substance.

2. Memories of earlier associations can surface with the word "tithe."

3. You feel a sense of great faith and trust is the path to walk when this procedure begins.

4. Surprises can occur when, after you give God 10 percent, you note how much money you have left to use.

5. Doubt may occur when the above experience is not immediate or when unexpected expenditures emerge instead.

6. You may be surprised at the wisdom and judgment you are using to manage the money you have been given.

7. You will enjoy the ease with which you are able to meet your financial obligations.

8. You will notice that your connection in God deepens and thus your spiritual life expands and your consciousness of wealth grows.

9. You will find that you get urges to send more than 10 percent to a number of places of spiritual nourishment.

10. You'll wonder how you've ever managed to survive without Tithing.

Invite God in to Our Giving and Finances

God will measure our grace with the same scale we use. If we offer a small sum, our blessing is also small. When we give graciously and generously, the reward of the Father is great!

This scripture shows without a doubt that you cannot out give God, you will also experience this. Here is another of II Corinthians 9:6-8: The truth is, God will pour out upon you his blessings and how to do that is very obvious to him.

"Bring all your tithes into the storehouse, that food may exist in My house, and try me now," says the Lord of hosts, "if I do not open the windows of the heavens to you, and pour out such blessing on you, the room may not be sufficient to receive it."- Malachi 3:10-Indeed, it asks that we prove it.

The problem is, many people 'try' tithing once and then give up because they haven't understood that tithing is a regular and consistent practice and also instead of spending time on their lives and finances with this spiritual principle constantly being active as you receive, you will give ten percent of your first fruits each time you receive. Gods Kingdom doesn't require a windfall or one off, God's Kingdom requires your constant faith. God says HE won't only pour out HIS blessing on you, but HE will revoke the devourer for your sake, and not let your hard work go in vain! (Malachi 3:11)

Do you know how important it is for you to let the Almighty God fight for you instead of fighting your own battles?

I know right now what you're thinking, perhaps, "This sounds fantastic, but I really don't know how I am supposed to pay my tithe, I cannot afford to pay my bills." What you're doing is paying your creditors and taxes, feeding your relatives, and seeing if enough is left to tithe. I can guarantee that if you manage your budget this way, you will never be adequate to tithe.

The first thing you have to do is tithe, that is the very first thing, that is where the power comes from.

The ten percent comes right from the edges. You give God the first seed, the first ten percent, before you do something else. That is the commitment. This is the right budget order: then take a seat, pay yourself, look after your family, pay your creditors and bills, you will be surprised in how things work out. As you stay committed, amazing blessings will occur in your experience.

If this month you are unable to pay all your creditors, you may choose to give letters to those you cannot pay and you can each pay a portion of the outstanding amount depending on the total bill amount. You will also learn to live without things you once thought important, a powerful financial wisdom and sixth sense overcomes you and you move into alignment. You will know it once it appears, that is the connection with the divine mind in your experience.

But here's the fascinating thing:

Get ready because you are about to witness financial miracles. How is it going to work? I don't know how with you really. I just know it works. I wasn't a good tither when I was stuck in debt. I just ran out of money before I got to the end of paying my obligations.

Once I learned how important tithing is, I knew I would not refuse anything. I sent out my tithe before I did anything else when I got my bill. I sent out money for the tithe if I was given any money.

I wrote a tithe check if I did a side job and got a little extra. Whatever — If I didn't sleep, if I didn't have energy, if my water was turned down — If I thought I would be starving and truly I never had any of that to think about. I have always been fed, I have happily paid my bills and had much more to live on.

Beyond everything, I could imagine, God blessed me. I am shielded when emergencies occur and my kingdom is built to prosper and prosper others.

People came out of the blue and gave me money. Someone randomly approached me and asked me to work freelance for them. I've never overlooked something that I wanted, I've done without some fluff, and things I didn't even need. But I had everything I wanted and more. I noticed that God was teaching me that my tithing benefited and blessed others who give too me and it will for you too. I feel truly accepted as a minister of teaching ancient principles in modern life. But this book, is dedicated to your local person, place or organization where you receive your spiritual help, support and inspiration. This book is about expanding spiritual places for the benefit of humanity everywhere.

If you're not tithing, begin now. Check your intentions, however. God loves a cheerful giver. Don't tithe out of service. Tithe because you love God and thank him for all the blessings you have recieved. Jesus requires you to be blessed by Grace. You encourage him to do that when you tithe, by the expansion of the Kingdom here on earth. What is the Kingdom? The place where our spiritual food is, such as the teachings of God and universality, love, wisdom, forgiveness, giving, friendship and nature. It is where the tools are kept to enhance our own spiritual growth and expansion.

The Bible tells us that God owns all the riches of the earth. He asks us to return ten percent of our profits to Him. However, some faithful still disregard this order to denounce or they depend on godless advice that discourages generous donation. No investment strategy will, however, compare to God's financial master plan. If we faithfully tithe, the Father will grant us generously.

God's plan varies from the will of the universe. Secular philosophy helps us to accumulate the greatest wealth. The reasons are self-serving, such as meeting our wishes and trying to ensure financial security. Stagnant and slimy water is created by a pool with no inlet or outlet.

Money can produce a similar and unhealthy outcome. An individual who does not manage the way with God will inevitably waste financial resources. A self-centered approach to finances decreases the quality of life of an individual and also creates tension within families.

The Lord is generous to His followers. We should not consider ourselves as holding tanks for our self-serving desires. Rather, we need to be platforms for good work, ready to share and inspire others.

In God's wisdom, the faithful receive to send, the faithful receive to give. You and I should use our resources for our needs and wants, but we have to donate to our faith, our worldwide missions, and help others who have financial difficulties learn to connect with Gods blessings. Better people are blessed, abundant, healthier, calmer, and much more happier and confident.

Luke 6:38 reads, "If you give, you will receive. Your gift will return to you entirely, will be pressed and shaken down to make room for more, and it will run.

No matter how big you give or how small you use it, it will be used to calculate what is given back to you." Choose to see your bank account as a reservoir instead of a pipe. Then watch the Father supply everything you need abundantly.

Here are four benefits that can be obtained from tithing:

-Abundance. Prosperity comes from offering one-tenth to the Lord, monetarily and otherwise.

-- Security and Protection. He controls your supply with Him as your spiritual boss. The Father kindly offers everything you need when you give back. He will protect you from all who seek to devour you, he will deal with your enemies on your behalf.

-- Demand. Don't try to find out if you can afford to give to the Lord if money is tight. The budget will not operate on paper, but if you are compliant and faithful, you will encounter his provision. –

- Personal witness. Following the master financial plan of God will bring you happiness, joy and peace. The changes in your life will provide you with a great opportunity to bear witness to the blessings offered by biblical observance.

2 Corinthians 9:7 reads: "Everyone must make a mind of himself how much he ought to give; do not give willingly or in answer to pressure; for God loves the giver that gives gladly."

Don't fall into the trap of building up money, believing more will buy you happiness. For example, look at the lives of some rich people. Most of them have no absolute friendship, true harmony or enduring happiness.

Be patient.

Despite the repercussions, you cannot break the orders of the Lord. Malachi 3:8-9 reads, "Should men cheat God? You cheat me! But you ask, 'What do you mean? When did we cheat you?'" You cheat me of my dungeons and my gifts. "

A decision not to tithe means sacrificing the four-fold benefits associated with giving: wealth, security, provision, and personal witness. The orders of our Father are for us to remit a one-tenth of what He has provided to us.

Blesses Those Who Give to You

Are we always more fortunate to give than to receive? Why, then?

If we look at our world's overall image, it's no exaggeration to suggest that if we had more resources and fewer people who were willing and put another way, fewer of those who have their hands set to the point of greed, which contributes to a complete mindset of themselves and myself.

In these conditions, the interests of others are not taken into account. Self sacrifice is not even a part of your personal ideology, so it cannot be evident in your actions. You don't understand how you can be honored to send. Egoism has stolen the happiness that they would get when they think about others.

I'm older, born first, second, and then me with God's trinity. I have to admit that in this order there is, and has always been, a blessing. Blessing arrives first in this trinity and not in the opposite trinity, then others, when it is necessary, and God if it suits into my theory.

Unfortunately, in the 1960s and 1970s, we entered the "me generation" and sadly this attitude had decades to refine itself so that other people's thinking is completely excluded from the thought-process.

Donors and givers of our world offer happiness and blessings not only to others, but to themselves as well. Giving up pure motivation to want to make another person happy and blessed, gives the giver happiness and blessings. You are therefore truly more fortunate to give than to receive.

People who hurt must become one with Karma also. Sadly, many times more people are hurt than those who are reserved or inclined to give. When we look around, we can see many people who need to be helped, many times just a kind word can be a blessing.

They will not know what anyone in their lives has to deal with. Therefore, seek to come out of yourself and give, so that you can spread the blessings in you and feel the joy. Find someone by giving today you will bless. Be imaginative when you give and see how happy you are when you give.

You can give without love, but you can't love and not give, to display His love. God blesses us to show us His love. He blesses us. No rich man, who loves his children, leaves them in need, so our father, who loves you and is the richest, will not leave you in need. All God does for you is out of His devotion.

God grants you authority to harvest the riches that He promised to your fathers (Abraham, Isaac, and Jacob)-Deuteronomy 8:18. God told Abraham in Genesis 12:2-3 that he would make him a great nation and that all the families of the world were blessed by him.

To establish the new nation and fulfill the covenant, God gave him Isaac and blessed it with new riches to sustain the covenant from generation to generation.

Abraham was the father of all Christian believers by Christ-Galatians 3:14. All Christians are now entitled to share with God and Abraham the blessings of this agreement. So in your life, God is obligated to affirm this covenant as the faithful giver; you are to be rewarded by Abraham because of your relation with Christ.

The people did not succeed in Haggai 1:4-10 because they left the house of God in ruin and proceeded to carry out God's work, and the heavens maintained its wife over them, and the earth brought no fruit to them.

That means that when God thrives, He wants you to use some of it for His work. You will use this to spread the Gospel and make Jesus' name a household name, to allow souls to be obtained into the Kingdom of God.

Winning the soul is God's desire, though His will to kill no one is not His. 2 Peter 3:9. Therefore, when God blesses you, He wants you to use part of it to satisfy His desire of heart to save all mankind-1 Timothy 2:4.

Because you may be a blessing-the Lord blesses you also-Genesis 12:2. In 1 Timothy 6:18 God commanded the rich to give to God when you give to the poor, and God gives back what you give

Proverbs 19:17 and when God pays back, you can be sure that He pays the fee, which goes beyond your idea, according to His size. Therefore, if you are born in your head, then you are a candidate for the blessing of Heaven.

Another solid purpose God blesses is to provide for you in all your needs, in accordance with Christ Jesus' riches in glory (Philippians 4:19), and you know that He is abundantly glorious.

The pipe that carries cold water is first cooled before the recipient, and before you can be a blessing God hopes that you should offer of what you have not -2 Cor. 8:12-13. He doesn't want you to relieve others and get burdened, NO.

In Malachi 3:14-18, God proclaimed that He was about to specifically differentiate between the righteous and the wicked, between those who are of His service and those who do not adhere to Him and abundance is one of the devices he will use. He would save his own from the world's economic crisis. He must freely recognize them as His jewels.

Isaac sowed hundreds of times during the drought while some left the land because of God's blessing – Genesis 26:12. Today, God always does; faithful Christians shine while many are swallowed up. When God blesses you and shines upon you, you have the doors of your enemies - Genesis 22:17.

You succeed to the glory of Heaven. Poverty does not bring God's glory. This is why God adds financial blessings on a person to His blessings. God wishes to bless you so much that when people learn and see what He has made you, as a sort of blessing, they will tremble and glorify Him - Jeremiah 33:9.

Jesus said in John 14:13 that He added riches to Solomon, as God rewarded Solomon with wisdom. As the King of Sheba came to see Solomon's wisdom and wealth, no more spirit was there in her. She had no choice but to glorify Him, who made king Solomon, and gave him wisdom and riches—1 Kings 10:4-9. Your wealth gives honor to Him.

Of course, God is going to bless those who are called by His name for His reason and align your heart and intentions according to God's plan and intent so that you can share in Abraham's blessings.

Allows Greater Spiritual Help, Wisdom and Inspiration Throughout Other Spiritual Places

The more we know the extent and quality of the gifts of Christ, the more we will be found."- Mother Theresa.

In a conversation with a dear friend and colleague, the issue of wealth and prosperity arose. Given all media reports about the economic environment, she had a very successful year personally and in her company, a very intelligent woman and marketer as well as highly desirable goods and services for which customers would call for.

Many people simply compare the money in abundance and fail to consider any aspect of abundance, as well as money such as love, energy, health, the encouragement of friends and colleagues, good memories, wisdom and a willingness to forgive ....

To be prosperous means to give and receive abundance with joyful gratitude and modesty for your offerings and blessings.

Give what you want in your lives most for the pleasure of another prospering, NOT to get anything in return. The beauty of the world cannot be appreciated until you are able to share it with others.

It is the essence of the Doctrine of Abundance or of Prosperity's Divine Order. The spirit of this law calls on us to take steps to show appreciation for the abundance already reflected in our lives and the greater good which is yet to be brought about.

So, I asked her, "What else has made your financial year so successful and so abundant?"

She said two things which added to her success. The first one was to hear her inner encouragement, motivation and intuition to make business and life choices that matched with her mind. That's what I think is a key element in a good life-listening to your heart's calling.

Second?

She says, "Tithing is about saying thank you, which also starts with a certain appreciation in our attitude. Gratefulness is about tithing in our money, but also in our feelings, words, acts, energy, effort and possessions.

She reminds us to thank everyone for their caring, thankful heart, even if it's their role in our lives. As a sign of appreciation for what we already have, we tithe as a token of our appreciation and our confidence that more good comes to us.

Tithing is the way to prove to both God and ourselves that we are willing, ready and able to embrace this increased abundance. The word tithe is based on the word tenth, a strong rise is assumed to be. Through sharing the good we receive with God joyfully and selflessly, we attach to the river of abundance, and we increase our blessings tenfold, even a hundredfold.

You are not to see the tithe as an obligation, it should be viewed as a constant opportunity to connect with the divine blessings of God for you and all you touch with its power." Tithing should not be viewed as a duty or obligation, but it is an act of faith. Tithing can be regarded as love offerings, free will gifts or a blessings that are freely offered, without any repayment. No matter the size of the donation, its truly about the purpose and intent of the offering and what it does for the spiritual you give it too.

All that is freely praised is multiplied and returned to you in an awaited and unforeseen way- by the Divine Rule of Prosperity that are hosting your continued good.

Do you refrain from sharing because you think you won't have enough?

Scarcity of thought and knowledge of poverty are continually blocking the influx of wealth, resources and opportunities into your lives that the World wishes to offer you. Picture more happiness, more love, health and energy, more independence, peace of mind and time to be with your people and your loved things.

Consistent tithing practices will improve your inner wisdom, confidence, wellbeing, prosperity, relationship fulfillment, spiritual connection and enable your openness to obtain what you really need without fear or expectation.

Give thanks with gratitude rather than anger, sorrow, disappointment or in the hope and anticipation of recovering. Give without strings attached, as you offer every heart gift.

Imagine what you would share with others then?

Who are you going to tithe to?

Give those who spiritually feed you freely and generously. Your local spiritual centers, leaders, teachers and mentors are excellent places to start. Personally, I also give money for friends and colleagues who have supported me with healing sessions, business advice and expertise, but my tithe comes first.

I always love giving gifts to my local Charities that feed families in the region so that they do not starve, But my tithe is always paid first. Sit down with someone who gives you divine inspiration, joy, support and comfort. Make sure you give your first tithe to them.

Do so with love and appreciation for 10 weeks to test it. When I started, I give myself a year to test it. I now could never not tithe.

Open your spirit, mind and body to accept all the abundant gifts, blessings and miracles that flow to you. Look forward to other ways of coping, a smile from a stranger, a new client, an email from a happy customer for your contact, a new business opportunity.

Check your blessings everyday in a newspaper and keep saying "thank you." For every love offering you receive and share freely when you are prompted to bless another.

What comes back may not be in the form of money at first. You can receive ideas, tools, links to others, for example, that improve your financial situation in the long run. Be open to the wonderful ways that the World meets your needs as you open your heart and checkbook in confidence and appreciation.

Chapter 8

Why Businesses Should Tithe?

Around 80% of the wealthiest people in the US have been able to do so by developing their own companies. The Millionaire Mind valued the "investing in my own business" as relevant for its success as 87% of the millionaires surveyed.

If any of you can only imagine the concept of owning your own company, you must know that less than 100 years ago, 85% of the US population owned their own company.

The definition of the employee and what it entails today is fairly modern, and our whole education system is structured to build workers and not contractors. No wonder many people have such trouble thinking about owning their own company!

Just don't think any business, including Ford, General Motors, General Electric, Microsoft, Apple, Google, would be in our capitalist system, unless there were someone who had the idea and bravery to break out on their own. Somewhere, occasionally something started with a lonely businessman. Ok, why not?

For you and your business, God has the unique idea.

Your business concept is to quickly build a cash machine so that, after your tithe, offerings and family commitments, you can use the money to invest in another object or to invest in real estate or even to start other businesses.

Your company will be your seed capital to invest in the Lord's work and promote other opportunities for investment for you and your family. Develop a business to generate revenue and use that revenue to increase income streams. This is what the wealthy do.

They build companies and business undertakings and use the money to invest in and grow more properties and viable investments.

Businesses would be the first way to supply the financial pipe, and your own business plays a significant role in your entire wealth growth strategy. We don't want to create a business that will be on the net for two years before profit is made. We haven't got time for that. We want a sustainable company that can make a profit quickly, and we'll talk about how.

Remember Deuteronomy 8:18 which says, "Remember, I pray you, the Lord your God, because he gives you power, that riches then become our own."

This is a way for us as individual believers to accumulate wealth rather than work for another and create the wealth of the business you are with. God will reward and give the employee a favor for promotions and bonuses in their business, but the employee works for money instead of merit.

Most of our parents who grew up in business told us to go to school and to graduate so that you can find a career with good benefits. They didn't know, but they helped us to become workers.

As we discussed earlier, workers are not second-class people. I'm just describing some differences between the two in terms of approaches for wealth creation. I recommend that everyone start their own company, even if you retain your full-time jobs while you build up your own business.

Everything is wrong with a steady paycheck unless it interferes with the ability to generate real money. Wealth is always sacrificed for protection, and the need for protection is rooted in fear. It is why more entrepreneurs are not forming their own companies.

The greatest fear is that we cannot depend on a steady paycheck. We were brought up to think that a stable paycheck is a normal way of generating revenues, and it can be a foundation for this kind of thinking which prevents us from being entrepreneurs and starting our own businesses.

Once again, if you're an employee right now, thank GOD you have a job and perform your work to the best of your ability. Your job may only be a foundation and training ground for your own company.

I have the need to do it because I don't want someone to say, 'Oh, Dane said that I would start my own business and I told my boss to shove it!' No, if you recall, during the first teaching of this series I discussed how you don't want to run out of work to start your own company.

Keep your full-time job as you start your own part-time company. Don't leave your work until you have ample revenue from your own business to cover your salary at the moment. In the same way, if you develop your own company on your hands, please be ethical and reasonable to your present employer.

Today, there is a distinction between an organization and a job. Many self-employed people still have jobs; they've only moved from job to jobs and they're still getting paying for their time. The aim is to build people and processes so that the business can operate without you. Own a system and have people working for you in that program.

Remember, the aim is to work more intelligently rather than harder. Working hard for your money may be important just when you start, but it should be temporary. If you are paying for your time only, you hamper your chances of creating wealth until you are able to double or maximize yourself.

Allow Yourself and Your Business to Partner with God

Tithing is good, its a wonderful tool used by virtually every productive individual. Tithing won't make you bad, it makes you generous, blessed and kind. Tithing will make you wealthy. Many affluent people donate to causes, churches, charities and they pay for their tithe and that's why they have become so rich. Read on as I explain why tithing would make you rich.

Tithing is a practice applied over thousands of years. Farmers will tithe a percentage of their crop to god per harvest in order to achieve prosperity on their farms.

As far as I know, the first written account of the tithe is in the Bible, but even though you are not a Christian tithe, it will extend to anyone who wishes to be wealthy.

1. Tithing Opens up Your Mind

Let's begin with a scientific view, so everyone can relate to it and understand it. I watched recently a TV news show that spoke of the benefits of non-spiritual tithing. They explained the act of tithing is good for your soul because it tricks your mind into thinking it is more than enough. This trains your mind to look for more money-making opportunities to give you more.

It's a little chaotic, because you need to give first before you get. Yet once you continue to give, you become more open mentally to more possibilities.

2. In offering and being generous, you are tipping the scale between giving and taking in your favor. In giving a church at least 10% of your income regularly, you are like a farmer who plants the crop. When a farmer sows seeds to the ground, he does not anticipate anything. It's an act of wisdom and faith.

He does so because he feels he will earn one hundred times the yield of what he has sown. The farmer would not be wise to expect harvest if he hadn't given any seed to the seedling cycle, and if we haven't tithed would we expect a financial harvest. By tipping the give-and-take scales.

3. Tithing Opens Heavenly Love On Your Life

Tithing opens up God's control over your lives. It is said that God will do more with your 90% than with your entire 100%. We allow God to do HIS work in our life by giving our money over to his kingdom. You can trust him with the small 10% to bless the remaining 90% and to increase your income, thus so increase your giving.

4. From a Being perspective we know it is said, "God does not need our money, but when we offer, we do a lot for both ourselves and the kingdom."

Tithing keeps us being in financial connection with the spiritual eternal side of ourselves. Some people get rich when they are not connected financially to our spiritual side, because they are never generous and do not give a dime to others unless it benefits them. The thing is that they are still unconnected with the spiritual financial at the end of the day, and that's no way to enjoy life.

Tithing protects you and it teaches you to be a compassionate person. The only way to live is to be compassionate. "You live with what you get, but by what you give you live." Some of the best memories I've had is when I supported people generously. Tithing keeps you from being lazy and losing one of the greatest delights (helping others).

5. The law of attraction states that whatever you think you are attracting and if you think "I have insufficient capital" you generate more circumstances to say "I have insufficient capital."

Through tithing, and doing so happily, you think of "I have more than enough," and you create more circumstances to say "I have more than enough." The law of attraction is still working, and tithing is a method we can use in telling God and the universe that we want more than enough in our circumstances. You would of course draw this to yourself by doing so.

Your next step in becoming abundant (after having of course the tithe) is to increase your financial intelligence by education, though you will receive a much deeper understanding of money through tithing it is smart to learn about money. You will be able to get more return on investment by educating yourself about finance, and you will be able to earn more with less labor and less risk.

Detach Yourself from Attachment with Money Knowing God Will Always Provide

Money isn't what most people expect it to be, and that's why they don't have any. The main thing you have to change in your money mindset is that money is stagnant, because it isn't. Money isn't like rocks, but most people treat it like this.

Money flows, money grows, and money goes, if you think otherwise, you have not really understood the energy of money. You most probably want the money to flow and expand and it does just that, the energy of money is active: money is a way of thinking. All abundance is. I describe wealth as an improvement in everything you care about. Wealth to me is not just money and it isn't figurative either.

Wealth for me is happy relationships that are deep, fun and nurturing, wealth for me is living the life I choose in alignment with my intentions, wealth for me is growth, expansion and expression.

Did the day it reached our door come in a million pound package? I doubt that. You must work with it, you must enjoy the life we choose to live, and above all you must set your mind in the right direction for you, and this is the way to be in its flow.

The rich don't garrison their money; they invest it, they put their money to work for them. Cash does not increase like relationship if you squeeze it to death. Some feeling of shortage or fear of loss is like squeezing. Ships sink in tight grips.

I know all these little truisms are cute, but they are real, especially about money. Since money is a feeling, a human illusion created completely temporarily on the beach, like sand. Go to the mint to see how millions to billions of dollars are lost every day only because they are worn out and you can imagine the flow to do that.

Webster describes illusions as actual, but temporary. When you understand this intangible essence of money in a great way, you will lose your will to hold it so tightly.

That is when you see that you can't keep something that doesn't last.

We can do it for a while, but getting detached from all permanent ideas in relation to money helps you to increase it. Such a detachment is the start of your cash flow.

Think about it. Money is fluid like water. When you dam it, what happens to a pond? All kinds of bacteria and algae grow to such an extent that everything gets choked.

Think of this too: if you think of money as being eternal, and have too much of it always, you're still right about what you believe, like everything else in the World.

Would you want to be sure about that, does that give you your confidence in growing it?

All the money you've got is in it?

So how will it grow?

So how's it going to flow?

Do you like to keep your relationship the same?

Never growing? Never being more satisfied?

I would like to say that your answer to that question would be a resounding "no." And why are you handling the flow of money in this way?

As if holding on tightly and not investing, this will somehow benefit you. It doesn't. This takes you out of the rhythm and into stagnation.

My first question is: "Why?" How can I let go? What am I investing my money in?

I always respond the same way, and I know that many don't like that response, but that's the nature of the facts. It is what it is, and in the uncertainty of finding out, you will be pushed out of your comfort zone into the field of progress where more transaction will take place and more development takes place.

The material world is constantly evolving with the minds of men and woman, and nothing stays the same. You can guarantee that investment into the areas that are both constantly needed and evolving will yield you return's at some point. Investment into learning the ancient principles that have stayed the same throughout the generations will also teach you about the very foundational power of the universe.

Because the fact is, I have no idea how you can let go or decide what you're going to invest in so that your money grows. You can only make these choices, and that's what it should be. What I do know is how to commit to the flow of money and to continue to use the powerful tithe in the face of any rise in wealth that you want in your lives.

Since your contribution also starts the cycle required for your advancement in any increase in wealth you seek and it is often without question that miracles come out of these commitments. I can't promise what the unique miracles would be in your experience. I can only say, "Go there and find out, the faster the better and be aware of how this principle works in your life."

Even before you continue to think that I do not have any specific "To do" ideas, I have one. One of the most common and efficient method of getting into the flow of money is to tithe.

What is created is the mentality and spirituality of abundance in both physical and spiritual reality and in this collection of "having enough to give it away" emotions, and miracles of increased richness occur in that abundant discussion.

I saw this reality so frequently in practice, I won't even attempt to explain why it works so well. Possibly I don't know why, only that it does. But I also don't know how electricity works so well, but that doesn't mean that I'm not always willing to use its flow to my benefit! You could do the same thing.

When you think you don't have enough money so you can't tithe, that's when you need to tithe more so that you can get out of the mind "I haven't enough" and into the mind "I have so much that I can still contribute ten percent of my income and do more than ever before." That is faith. That is how we become as tithers.

Realize that through our thoughts we have our own effects. I like the amazing outcomes most of all by being in-the-flow, that which leads to an increase in my income, wisdom, power, generosity, compassion, love and protection.

Now that you are thinking in a rich way, the one you must obey is The Detachment Law says that to effectively attract something, you must be detached from the consequence. When you are attached, you generate negative emotions of fear, doubt or desire that will really attract the opposite of your desire.

You work in a place of anxiety, fear and doubt instead of serenity, confidence and faith. Certainly, there are moments when negative emotions need to be felt and achieved, but the dominant emotions should be positive.

Let go and let God. Everything you desire can be achieved by detachment, because detachment is based on trust in the absolute grace of God and the knowing that He works through you and together with you for the greater good. To be connected is to know that all good is of God, because through our good actions through our spiritual awareness, we offer far more benefits than we could possibly know to humanity, with the power of God.

It is God who is doing it through you and through other things in your life, so you have nothing to hang on to, only have the right faith and let God do it.

The ease and perfection of practice depends entirely on how much we avoid depending on the consciousness. You will erase your conscious mind and allow the take over of your subconscious mind. The pilot and the autopilot cannot simultaneously operate the aircraft. You must let go to allow God to take over.

Detach is to let the universe manifest your desire in the best way for you. When you are detached, your desires manifest much more quickly.

To be attached means to be weakened, because you give it your strength over what you are adding too, looking through limited perception. Most miracles come unexpectedly; they are supernatural events that come out of reality we cannot perceive. When you look outside sources to fulfill you, you give away your power.

When you look for strength and joy outside of yourself, you make something other than your true self your source. Be disconnected, realizing that you have no control over something you disconnect from, but you have absolute power over it.

Deeper Financial Wisdom and Greater Financial Decision Making

Most people are searching for spiritual financial guidance with a complex and uncertain environment that will help to bring stability in these dangerous times.

Regardless of whether you just begin your journey, want to recover after a disaster, or simply seek advice to create a better financial future, there are basic ancient laws that still apply and will thrive you when followed.

Too often, when sustainable prosperity comes from a solid and properly built base, we want fast solutions. True financial independence is accomplished one step at a time, because the wisdom of the financial independence will need to make itself known to you in a way you understand it.

"Good plans and hard work lead to riches, but hasty shortcuts lead to poverty." Proverbs 15:22

Financial security is still possible, even in the most challenging and unstable environments, by following this straightforward spiritual advice and smart money management tips.

1. Create Financial security on Biblical Principles Philippians 4:19

It is easy to have faith in our own wisdom and success during a time of prosperity, and when we face a crisis or face a risk to our safety in the future, we start to recognize the true vulnerability of our financial base.

Sometimes it seems like we're living in a world where financial prosperity is merely an illusion-the mythical house on the sand like produces fleeting illusions of grandeur, which cannot survive the storms of existence. We assume that we have done all the right things so that we are ruined by the scrap of badly formulated financial plans.

Based on Ancient Scripture principles is the only path to true financial stability. We have to "cast of our own wisdom" (Proverbs 23:4) and rely on the guidance of the One who is committed to guiding and meeting our needs.

Changing the way you view your finances by following spiritual guidance is the first step towards achieving the financial success you have always dreamt of.

2. Be a Wise Manager. 1 Corinthians 4:2

The road to financial destruction is typically filled with bad decisions, unwise spending habits and inadequate budgeting. "In addition it needs stewards to be considered faithful and trustworthy." You must take care of your finances and create a strategy to manage your spending and achieve your objectives in order to achieve financial success.

You have to be a wise steward: Developing a detailed budget is essential to keeping your financial situation clearly visible. Knowing where your money goes helps reduce reckless expenditure, avoid debt, and keep you in charge of your finances.

a. Eliminating debt – Debt is never healthy, and too much debt can lead to stress in all aspects of your life. Proverbs 22:7 reminds us that the creditor is the borrower's employee and real financial freedom is offered by the measures taken to simplify your budget and to reduce or relieve yourself of debt.

So a lack of debt would eventually lead to more wise investment funds available, which will work for your future. If your budget is absolutely daunting, one of the many debt reduction options available will help.

b. Develop smart spending habits – good habits usually carry good results and smart money management is important.

Excessive use of credit cards, deferred payment plans, vehicle leasing or home loans can sound like promising ways of making desired purchases, but high interest rates and declining prices could make you feel a mountain of debt and a high financial burden. Consideration of purchases and the avoidance of impulse purchases will help you avoid difficult situations.

c. Prepare for the unforeseen – Unforeseen costs will disrupt your clean budget and cause tremendous stress. If you can put a little money in an emergency fund every month, you will be better prepared and ready when problems occur.

3. Seek wise guidance. Proverbs 15:22

The development or writing of a financial plan is an important part of future financial stability. Proverbs 15:22

The development of a financial plan is a crucial factor in the financial security of the future. Consulting a financial planning specialist will help you set targets, remain focused and decide wisely.

Choosing the correct investment can be frustrating, and a golden chance can easily be a catastrophic error, so we avoid it completely all too often. Seek advice from financial advisors who understand Bible values will allow you to make intelligent investments that suit your goals and provide future protection.

Christian financial advice based on the Bible will motivate you to get your finances together and enjoy true financial freedom.

Everyone may claim to be competent in industry, but not everyone carries the financial skills to consistently sustain performance. Financial responsiveness cannot be obtained by means of an online certificate or a web planning programme.

It is learned from experience or, if not from hands, from lessons acquired from plays, bruises and all, and it triumphs. A good online business owner also comes from listening to the stories of the right people.

Focus On Serving Your Customers and Staff, Trust God To Make All Else Good

Significant amounts of money, time and energy are spent on new customers. Nevertheless, a large part of these customers are constantly lost.

Treat your client as the most important person in your business. No clients will equal No sales; No sales will equal No income. Acquiring new customers can be expensive and time consuming; it's much cheaper to support existing customers and provide them with more of your services.

Therefore, it is important to do what you can to retain your customers. Most companies 'romance' the prospect into a customer. But after the Honeymoon period full of many obligations and a lot of attention has come to an end, complacency is slowly diminishing and focus has been potentially distracted by another 'lover.'

"To be on par in terms of value for money and quality just gets you into the game, it is service that wins the game."

Below are four principles that will allow you to retain a customer:

The Four Principles

1: Love your customer as yourself

"The greatest revelation my generation has ever had is that people can alter their lives by altering their attitude." The secret is good customer service.

Can you and your employees have the customer's desired service?

There is no common support system for customers. Customer standards also differ and their tolerance rates vary. If you want to "love" them, you need to know your customer.

How do you answer customer complaints?

Do you get defensive or listen carefully to the argument, explain it and then check it before you respond?

Are you tracking consumer complaints?

Know, clients speak to other clients. It is reported that an dissatisfied customer talks about your service to at least nine others, while a pleased customer talks hardly unless asked. It is helpful to keep your clients happy (loved) by changing your attitude towards clients.

2: Correct your understanding immediately

I am sure you do your best to please your clients, like most company managers and owners. Nonetheless, this cannot always be interpreted by consumers. They may have changed their view after a series of mild negative experiences. Truth is perception.

In order to correct this idea, you must act immediately. Simple talk and promises won't help. You will have to prove that things have improved to be preferred again. One of my clients performs regular customer satisfaction meetings to find out and respond on consumer expectations.

Another approach is for the sales representatives to frequently ask the client, "How we can please you better?"

3: Ensure the right hand knows what your left hand does.

While one area can serve them, another area may fail. It may even be the subcontractor who offers bad service. When I was in a senior management role for a big company, I had to make sure that customers expected the right quality of service, timeliness and consistency of delivery, accurate and timely invoicing, etc.

If the account team sent out incorrect invoices, consumers were 'thinking.' While it was beyond my remit, I had to consider the complaint and do so. You must learn and let each team know how their service affects the view of the company by the customer.

4: Create a customer service strategy, train the staff rigorously and carry it out.

If you are not committed to customer service, the employees will not likely stick to it. Inclusions in a Customer Service Program are essential:

1. Personnel mentality (the consumer is sovereign and must be handled as one)

2. Telephone etiquette-Consumer Speaking

3. Care standards (specific, observable, realistic, appropriate, timely, accepted by all)

4. How people train and track customer service should be done on a regular basis both to highlight their value and to educate them in all aspects of customer care and high quality of service.

Each new employee will also be educated as part of the orientation process in customer service. Your current clients are your biggest asset. Serve them well and you're going to keep them and your company will prosper.

It is easy to determine a tenement for workers since they earn a paycheck. This is more complicated for company owners because there are so many organizational structures, revenue streams and accounting requirements.

As a result, company owners are left to define their own strategies for measuring a tenth. I hope this effort to recognize factors for business owners is the start of a discussion which helps many to do what our Lord has called us into question in Malachi 3:10-12:

Bring the whole tithe into my shop, that my house may have food. Test me here," says the Lord Almighty, "and see if I don't open the floodgates of heaven and give it so much blessing you won't have enough room for it.

Test me. I will not allow pests to devour your crops, neither will the vine in your fields that bear fruit," says the Lord, the All-Powerful. "Then shall all the nations call you blessed, for yours will be a pleasant earth," says the LORD of hosts. (NIV) Over-arching considerations As business owners, we have tackled these problems and faced a number of challenges.

A tenth of all things from the earth, whether grain from the ground or fruit from the trees, belongs to the LORD; it is holy to the LORD," says Levitius 27:30-33. If a man raises a tenth, he has to add a tenth of the value. The whole tenth of the flock—each 10th animal passing under the shepherd's staff—is holy to the Lord.

He should not select the good out of the bad or take substitution.' (NIV) This has been told to farmers and there are adjustments that we have to make, because we apply the principle in the economy today. But what it doesn't say is to tithe what's left of all your fields produce after you have paid everything else every year.

Every man must give what he determined, not reluctantly or under coercion, to give from his heart, for God loves a joyful giver.) Instead of treating our tenth as a bill to pay, we are happily considering it as a luxury to give. Bringing to our church is also my favorite worship as it is my visible offering to our caring and gracious God, his kingdom and his faithful.

Most company owners want to make their company a "tithing business." The optimal "first fruit" model (based on gross profit) is to have 10 percent of the net book profits before tax. This measure would include all income sources.

Considerations:

Possession of single land. Alone owners might think they would use their net profit as their tithing basis. Nevertheless, some tax benefits may decrease the amount on this line in a way that it is no longer "first fruit."

Relationship. A majority of partners will agree that they are a tithing company. If not, individual partners might base their business tithe on something other than what the tithing principle is. All partners should agree prior to tithing, how this is to be done.

Accrual accounting basis

Accrual accounting refers to the allocation of revenue and expenditures. Assuming that both revenue and expenditures are considered by this system, the tithe will also be focused on book net profits.

Calculation of the personal income of the business owner

A company owner will personal tithe 10% of the income from all sources before taxation.

Both forms of income earned from the company (paychecks, leases, interest, rentals, etc.) and other sources are included. Any investment that has changed value – up or down – but has not yet been realized is exempt from this estimate.

Corporate owners are warned not to treat the tithe like a levy. U.S. tax law requires certain costs to be charged by the corporation which are simply personal costs. However, when considering the spirit and intent of the challenge of God to tithe, these expenses should be backed up to achieve a corresponding sum of "first fruit."

The goal is not to live by a strict rule but to live a life that represents our Lord's generosity. He asks us to tithe and to live with his works generously. Those suggestions will help us deal with the challenges, make a start and to live the compassionate lives we aspire for

Examples Of Businesses Who Tithe

A young man answered the call to become an African missionary, but noticed that his wife was unable to endure the African climate after further study. She got really sick.

He was heartbroken, but he returned home prayerfully and was determined to make all the money to spread the Kingdom of God around the world. His dad, a dentist, had begun to make an unfermented wine for communion service on his side.

The young man picked up the company and developed it until it took on massive proportions - its name was "Welch" whose family still manufactured "grape juice" He literally gave hundreds of thousands of dollars in offerings to the missionaries' work and really attracted the church of Jesus Christ.

Someone says the tithe is only for the wealthy. However, we have never heard of a wealthy man or woman starting to tithe, but we can name scores that started to tithe when people were poor and then became rich:

Mr. Crowell, founder of Quaker Oats Co.

Mr. Colgate-Colgate Soaps maker

Mr. Proctor of Ivory soap

Mr. Matthias Baldwin of Baldwin Locomotive Industry

R.G. Le Tourneau – creator of a large world moving business

Chapter 9

Why Governments Should Tithe?

The many tithes and offerings of ancient Israel were gathered by the priests and distributed by the Levites as social welfare administrators of their age. Those who handled the funds were known as righteous men, concerned with social justice issues. Those who gave and those who received could and did trust them.

Proud people are reminding us that we are a country of law and not animals and whose rules we follow except rich and foolish men's rules? People that studied law but do not understand justice. People who make laws for the good of others and people who use laws to gain power and position.

In ancient days, the minimum annual tithe was 10% at the start of harvesting. Increased income was effectively positive. If a person invested ten thousand in products, he knew God wanted him to give up 10% of ten thousand dollars.

It was a voluntary contribution, as the Scriptures said that refusing it from the poor is to rob God and rob God as a great theft and cause of curses. There was no civil penalty or judgment for those who refused the tenth because his life relied on divine grace.

Karma- He will be recompensed or missing according to his plays.

Today civil government pretends it can claim whatever it wants, from whomever it wants to build anything it wants.

Each day, more and more of those over whom they rule are increasingly conscious that leadership is in the opposite direction. The eyes closed by repeated indoctrination for several years gradually open to the weariness of compliant obedience and service.

In ancient times, no standing armies offered only a false sense of protection at large public expense to the detriment of both the rich and the poor. Trained militias allowed a man to render voluntary service a few hours a month before more was required in order to ensure social organization.

No major space exploration to be funded.

There is no debt liability that must be paid for interest. No skilled lawmakers claim that their exclusive services to the highest bidders are deserving of big salaries. No great infrastructure has been built, restored and maintained. Unlike charities, civil administration was easy, voluntary and inexpensive.

So what is rational or what is realistic doesn't matter.

Public officials are masters with the consent of the masters whom they supposedly represent and with the consent of their money masters. Roles are changed and new servants tell the new masters very little. In such a system, uncertainty is the only certainty.

The tithe was obtained in ancient times to ease the hardships of the needy. Today, we have a much greater global consciousness and tithes collected among the poor who are not specifically among us, but still much neither than the ones we used to find to be our own, our domestic poverty.

Because of the unmerited blessings of great wealth, rich nations have had over the past two centuries, more serves us if we are to display gratitude, disobey our wasteful habits and also help the third of us in abject poverty after providing the first fruits to Gods Kingdom.

A national spiritual government will spend no less than 10 percent of its annual revenue which will be the first 10 percent raised – to relieve the great demands of spiritual organizations in our nation.

Had that been the case over the last two hundred years over Spiritual Britain, the poor in Britain would not be motivated to crime and disharmony for a better life.

All that matters as a country for Britain is presence. Let's give the world a lovely photo hiding the underlying rot. The universe is much easier to fill than to enjoy it and to take care of or around it. Let comfort rule. It is time that someone else does the hard work. We're going to cheer them on.

The feeling conveyed in U.S. currency, "we trust in God," is just that. The national tithe is the indicator of trust. We can give any number, since we know that God does not only substitute what we give but multiplies it for both the giver and the receiver. The niggardly men in control are positive this is not so.

They just believe in their own "sacred" law and nature's resistance to good intentions. The illness of the nation makes medicine a development industry, an industry with low faith in God.

Believe it or not, it's a very serious matter with the guidance in the scriptures. Forget about the debate of tithing in the church.

Does the Bible allow us to give the government 10 percent of our increase?

As a small and intimate act, 'I' should have offered a tenth of my fortune, for that should be a sign of sincere gratitude. But I should have made a political move that looked like paying a levy.

Many biblical scholars regard tithe as the minimum duty and stress that sacrifices above and above the tenth reflect our heart's true purpose.

Enriches The Economy

As a consequence of what people hear about the economy, many of them cling to the last penny. You may choose to be influenced by the media or be a donor.

The rule of giving and receiving ensures that you earn more than you have contributed when you give back. This rule has been around for thousands of years. Even like the laws of physics are not politically bound, neither is the law of giving and receiving. The law works with precision and consistency.

Since 2012, I have been practicing this law and more recently, I have practiced it diligently and consistently. Over this time, I have faced challenges and opportunities, like most people and yet this Law of Giving and Receiving has never disappointed me once.

Every farmer practices this law every season. The farmer needs to "send" the seed to the land. The seed he has is nourishment. He could eat the seed, he planted it instead, and gave it away.

Yet as everyone knows, if you grow a kernel of maize, you won't get a kernel back. You're going to get some ears of maize back and every ear of maize is packed with kernels.

The Law of Giving and Receiving has been created to give you more than you give. What would be the point if you just got what you gave back? It'd just be a waste of energy.

This law is really very obvious when it comes to farming and planting crops. However, very few people see and understand that any of this legislation applies and as far as finances are concerned, there is both confusion and skepticism about this understanding because of the way it has been previously taught and understood.

Suppose a farmer has planted a maize field. He has "given" the soil seed. He will obtain back in abundance according to the rule of gift and reception. But what if he never goes to the field to pick his crop during harvest time? The law has not failed; there is his return. He didn't just go out and get it.

Some citizens only use this rule to be discouraged because they have not earned it back. This occurs for a variety of reasons. Many people give their crop and don't get it because they don't expect it or try it.

Many didn't get it because they're definitely tossing here a little seed and there a little seed, never really trusting that this divine principle works. They are inconsistent and very little seed is planted. Ask a farmer how well this will do during harvesting!

Many people were the perpetrators of the abusers of this Law by telling them that miracle outcomes would occur at night if they give them their check. Now I have no faith in the divine at all, because this is an everlasting law founded by the Almighty.

Nobody is entitled to say exactly when and how the section of it will be "sent." It is dishonest to tell people that, if they give their debt, it will be wiped out miraculously. It is the duty of God to carry His supply to you, however, as you do the rule of giving and receiving. That's his

Our job consists of three equally essential sections.

First of all, we commit to understand and accept this law. Test it for two or three months, and then you're sure.

Second, we sow seed regularly. Not sporadically, but truly whenever we get some production, we give it right from the top and we sow it in the best soil we know of. Most people want to "sow their seed" where good spiritual nourishment is given.

Third, we believe in a return and expect it. Our eyes are open, our heads open. Our ears are open. Our heads are open and our hands are free. That is the law of gift and reception. God will offer His provision to you, so you must go out and collect it. You will receive wisdom and protection.

In a poor economy, just note that this law has been around for thousands of years and it always works. It works. Not only that, but with great abundance, God produced this world. There is always plenty to send to his kingdom.

People debate how much somebody ought to give. Some preach that for ancient times the tenth tithe mentioned in the Bible was not applicable today. Now it sounds like a farmer telling a farmer that he planted the entire seed bag, but he is just planting part of it now.

There are numerous passages in the Bible as you have read some here that guarantee abundance if this Rule of Giving and Receiving is applied. One of them is from the book of Proverbs, a text full of wisdom.

It states in the eleventh chapter that "one man freely gives, but all the rich grows more, another refuses what he ought to give, and suffers only in want. A freeman will be enriched and one who waters himself will be fed." Give your time, your money, your talents and your skills. Do it with the right spirit and look forward to it.

Help Spiritual People, Places and Organizations Do More Good

If you work out of the spirit of abundance, you know what it offers in the world, and everything that you want or desire is ready and able to be given for you.

In our world, there is no shortage. The only position that is missing or bad is in the mind. Nothing is missing in the Universe. Everything is available in an infinite, inexhaustible supply. That includes money and prosperity. It includes love, forgiveness, happiness, power and protection. It includes giving and receiving and the power of our positive thoughts over our experience in reality.

One of the most effective ways to show the World is to tithe.

Tithing helps the energy of money to continue to flow and lets you avoid the feeling that you don't have enough wisdom and power over your money. In the land of supporters, you can't be a 'taker.' Our universe is built on the idea of contribution and contribution.

You shall receive as you Offer. You have to be a giver. Many of the wealthiest and most popular people have also been major donors. It's all the idea to plant and harvest. If you have never planted, you can't produce a crop. Sharing is the foundation of a successful success and prosperity program.

While sharing, many of the most popular people have realized the influence of tithing all the time. Personally, I believe it is the biggest secret you will ever find for success, achievement and personal wealth.

Tithing will go to your spiritual help center. It is an essential difference. Your tithe is to the true source of all that riches-the World. Wherever you receive spiritual illumination, you should tithe to it.

When we are happy to tithe and thankful for what we have, realizing that we already have everything we need, we will find our blessings.

In other words, don't sit there and wonder when is your return. It is necessary not to expect a return. You actually tithe and you know that your tenth will be returned to you soon, somewhere.

Tithing from a position of 'confidence' that all of your needs will be met frees you from the position where you 'expect' or need a return. Would you waste your time looking for a return if you have limitless resources? Probably not.

If you can take your tithe from a position where you feel like you've got infinite support and thanks for sharing it, you are in the place to receive and you will be aware of how the blessings come to you. In the financial circles, it is always said that you should first be paying for yourself and then putting the money aside for an emergency or an investment plan, that is smart, however, it is not for everyone, God will guide you to what is right for you.

Some assume that we live in a materialistic world of the "dog eat dog," where everything happens by chance, and where one must concentrate solely on their difficulty. It does sound crazy, but I know we can show that the world is not dead to spiritual principles and that it is very much alive.

On the other hand, as the well-known Cosmologist Ervin Lazlo said, "The Universe is an energetic, complex, and reactive place built for up tithing." You can start by aligning with the KARMIC Nature of the world and then pay 10% of your income to support others. Now, watch what's going on.

Our world is a virtual dream machine, which works for one key act: "giving." There are other ways to share, such as giving others your attention, support, and smiles.

I listened to thousands of people and I suggested it to thousands more. If they honestly gave money to someone, I do not know anybody, nothing happened. Nevertheless, many neglect this essential form of prosperity and some people need an explanation on how dining should work exactly, so I'll give you a short one.

I firmly know that if you are honestly practicing tithing, you can see for yourself how your life will improve. It will trigger the flow of synchronous opportunities and return blessings to you.

How the world works is designed to respond correctly to the act of giving. Also, by paying attention to what happens, you can prove this to yourself. It starts as a change in mindset that influences the kind of things happening to you in the world directly. Any time we communicate with others, this change in mindset will take place.

We must move our attention away from concentrating on what we can get by engaging with others and concentrate on what we can offer to the other person. This means remembering to ask consciously, "What can I say or do about the person in front of me?"

You can expect two things to come back if you change your attitude. You begin to reawaken your innate ability – your connection to an inner intuition that comes to you, and you wonder how I can support others. Then you get an intuitive hunch, feeling or picture, practicing how and sometimes with money you can support this guy.

Over time, intuitive skills are developed in order to effectively explain and address the intuitive advice you are looking for. Finally, it should sound almost obvious as though you are aware about your deeper spiritual awareness.

You need to feel more confident about what to do and what to do in any case. Aside from helping others, this enhanced intuition is a reliable inner support that directs you consistently on your best path to the most satisfying life.

Of course, from a quick transition into a more "private" mentality there is still plenty to be recovered. But there's more!

You will begin to see more positive returns as you bid. Since you want a good synchronicity with others, you can see more people move synchronously into your life. You can be there to provide useful information or to give money to a financial opportunity at the right time. The less money you have, therefore, the more important it is to tithe.

You will find that we appear to have interaction with people who practice similar behavior. This is the overall image of the karmic nature of the universe. When you are a donor, you attract other donors.

When you're a taker, you can see people taking you or exploiting you in your life, and it undoubtedly will cost you money. If you wish to be happy, begin with alignment and continue to be a conscious giver. To grasp how this concept works, remain aware of your interactions and then see how people can teach you synchronicity consistently.

Our life experience is incomplete. Everything that happens in your life, however, is not inherently a result of fate. At the beginning, we may be sick. It's not because of Karma but that you haven't managed to stop toxic illness.

For another scenario, we could be involved in an accident because we did not upgrade our intuitive results. These occurrences are not Karmic, but they arise when these problems have not yet been solved by human evolution. We shall therefore aspire to "trade" as our leading karmic agent and boost the quality of our lives significantly.

When you decide how much money you would like to spend, the fun part begins! You can intuitively wait and watch where you are led to give capital. It may take different forms.

In this way, the scriptures tell us that you can test this divine mechanism by giving and waiting fully for a return of Gods Blessings, although all will not be returned from the same source. Of the principal, that's sure! Stay open and don't miss something, be true to the shift in attitude.

Synchronously, someone then unexpectedly emails you for a good money cause. In this situation, you turn over this direction and become a mentor for more.

Tithing clearly has many social consequences. First of all, the divine plan aims to "send money" to help other people all over the world. The more we give, the more money we get, the more money we give.

If everyone in the world wants to give 10% immediately, there is plenty of money to solve all problems of humanity by beginning a new era of spiritual consciousness. In fact, it would not be a wasteful government to do so.

Via education, we will fully eradicate all hunger, clean the toxic contaminants from the environment and less destructively move towards a renewable energy system. Much of this is "better" organized.

Everything you have to do is agree individually to collaborate with a world to offer. You continually increase the motivation to make the world a much better place.

Chapter 10

Why We Should Teach Tithing People to Practice?

Tithing Is a Personal Experience

Tithing means giving 10 percent of your profits to a spiritual purpose (the tithe means "tenth"). Some people swear by tithing and consider it as an integral part of wealth formation.

Tithing benefits include: overcoming scarcity thought. Tithing allows you to grow a more abundant meaning. You are conditioning your subconscious to believe in abundance thought by giving 10% of your profits. This will make your money more accessible and responsive. You are more likely to encounter abundance if you consider abundance.

Supporting a dignified cause

When you use the money you tithe, you will support a spirituality that is important to you.

Acquire more money

As you gain more money, your amounts will also be increasing, so that your cause(s) receive more financial support. For certain people, this can be particularly motivating.

I honestly believe that some people get too interested in the actual activity of dining and lose sight of their true intent. We need to keep ourselves humble and thankful.

Take into account the true intention of tithing. The goal of the tithe is to serve the highest good of all. However, dining is only one of many ways of serving the highest benefit, definitely not the only way.

Many other forms are possible to support the common good. Any thoughts here: Give time, Donating time to a cause you find is worthwhile. Perform a service act.

Send facts

Write articles or start a blog to openly share your information with those who can benefit and profit from it.

Offer skills.

Using the skills to support those who can't afford it and those who don't have the skills.

Smile at people.

Today, give somebody a kind word. Recognize a job well done.

Help those around you. Let others know you're interested in them and there success and achievements.

Grant feelings. Do the best for everyone.

Pray or meditate for others if they have meaning for you.

Give a pat on the back, a smile, or a hug to someone. Grant yourself a massage. Offer exciting gifts.

Consider other ways to offer, it will be a lot more fun.

When I'm going to support the front end, I should support the back-end. I won't water those roots if the cause is rooted somewhere in violence, war, covetousness or other thought scarcity.

The reason you put into your donation is more important than the specific way of giving. Offer yourself in a way that makes you feel good, not guilty and if you have no viable outlet to offer that that fits your beliefs and makes you feel comfortable, then put the idea for a new outlet to offer into your life.

Attaining Consistency

One of my struggles was to strike a balance between giving and receiving. In the last year, I worked really hard on the side of giving and declined to receive a lot, this is not balance. However, my blessings kept returning to me one way or another.

For me now, this means welcoming more abundance into my life, but at the same time serving in the best way I can.

I don't worry about giving vs. receiving anymore. To me, they are truly the same thing.

There is a place where giving is normal and receiving is selfless. You will find and travel to this place in your own life.

As you do so, your lack of thinking will vanish, and your truth will float into a sense of abundance.

Teach People to Reflect On Their Experience with Tithing

Abram knew God and HIS words. He felt the presence of God as well as His deliverance. Abram knew he had nothing without Him. Giving God a tenth is a little recognition of what God offers us each day.

Sometimes we don't hear God as much as we would like. This doesn't mean he is not there. Note, God never changes. Heaven never changes. We are those who turn away from Him. Once we return to Him, God will be with us.

God tells us in Malachi 3:7, "Return to me and I will come back to you." (NIV) One of the best things about God is that when He comes to us, He comes in wonderful ways and by wonderful things.

Malachi 3:10 tells us that God will throw open the floodgates of the sky and pour out so much blessing that you will have no space for it if we are right in giving our tithe. (NIV)

Can we even believe that we have enough room for our blessings in an economy like that, in times of scarcity and lack?

God is a generous Father, and we become generous like him.

What are our attitudes?

Our Tithes and offerings should show our humble appreciation of the glorious mercy of God. He still loves us, even in our sin. Regardless of how wrong we were, He is always able to forgive and bless us.

Tithes and offerings should be freely given out of love. Amos 4:5 urges us to honor your gifts of free will-to boast about them and that's what you want to do. (NIV) How are we going to give?

Activities we normally enjoy are front of mind. If the tithe is not yet a front of the mind, we can motivate ourselves to get there.

In 1 Corinthians 16:2 Paul told the Corinthians that on the first day of each week you should put away an amount according to your incomes and save it so that when I come no collections are made. (NIV) Tithing is expected to come from the top of our profits. When it is first, there is no question about whether any money would be left after the bills.

God has given us our work, our willingness to do a job. First, we will show him our gratitude. Consider how many of our families, neighbors, and colleagues told us in the past year or two about the loss of their jobs. It could have been one of us. Jesus will continue to save and support us.

Although many faithful addressed the subject, my teacher has best summarized it. Will you choose a large blessing or a net blessing to determine what kind of blessings you need? How we offer it, is how we hope to receive it.

Jesus explained to us that in Luke 6:38 you will be judged by the scale you use. (NIV) Malachi warns us of our tithes and sacrifices being stripped of Him. We may not have been in alignment in the past with what God wants of us, but it's never too late to begin. Once we are ready, God is ready to take us out. Let's try to be outstanding in all.

God asks us in Malachi 3:10 to test him with the tithe and to see what he does in exchange for us. Let's take him on this word, let's take him up on the offer.

Tithing is the ethical custom of gifting 10% to where we are spiritually nourished. It aims to build knowledge of the Spirit as our One Source and demonstrate our abundance. If this is a new idea for you or you are in financial problems at the moment, it can trigger a lot of real fears.

Instead of confronting and coping with these concerns, it is common to simply dismiss the concept of tithe as 'stupid' or 'unreasonable.' Be mindful that you have these feelings. Most positive and spiritually based people use this activity as a way to continue their lives.

While there are financially wealthy people who do not tithe again and again, tithing provides a flow and sense of protection in our lives that cannot be ignored. Here are some suggestions for promoting the ethical practice of tithing:

1. Start Giving

When your tithing is new, it may take you some time to only give back money to where you are spiritually fed.

That is not the case for everyone, but for me it was a big move. I was completely new to the idea of tithing (and initially suspect).

It made no sense to me to give money away because I could barely make ends meet. At first, I had to release money gently. It essentially taught me to let go, this was a breakthrough for me. I don't see money the same way anymore, it is just a tool for me and has no power over me now but I have power over it.

3. When you earn taxes, please determine how much money you are returning.

Even if the sum seems big, I enjoy knowing that I will be able to give easily in the future. "This week I got £1000! I'll send £100 to my spiritual centre!" Try for a while if you are not here yet.

You can wonder how amazing it feels to give up ten thousand pounds. I imagine all the happiness, peace and security my £100 contribution brings to others. Practice this until it becomes a reality. It all begins with the mind and our intention.

4. Practice Consistency

You want to be giving the first 10% every time you receive. This is keeping in alignment with the universal spiritual law.

5. The aim is to give freely and joyfully, realizing that the world is abundant, this allows you to open your mind and awareness to the blessings you both give and receive.

Trust and know that what you offer is multiplied and abundantly returned to you. Prepare to give graciously and strive to receive graciously.

I urge you to study this custom if you are still not sure about tithing. Ask your inner spirit to provide you with resources to increase your understanding in meditation or prayer. The practice of tithing has helped me significantly shift my perspective on finance and that's practice.

Economies of Government Officials That Tithe

Tithing gives God's kingdom ten percent of what you receive. This should be given to God's house. Make sure that the house of God in which you have chosen to tithe is built on the word of God and for the betterment of the faithful.

Through this way the promises of God can be fulfilled exactly the same in your life. God says, take all the tithes into my storehouse so there's food and try me if I don't open the windows of the sky and pour out the blessing you have no space to receive.

The first thing you can do is tithe if you collect your paycheck or some other money. It tells God that before all else you bring him. This allows you not to be tempted to use the tithe for your personal requirements.

Regardless of what you need, first you can tithe and budget for the remaining 90%. It is a vision of sacrifice. God will bless you truly when your needs supersede your income and yet you have chosen to tithe. Only do that, realizing diligently that there is a day when you have more than enough.

Tithing is a symbol of God's worship in sacrifice. If you want to give it no matter how hard things are for you, it is always pushed. Today, he tells you that the situation is very temporary. He's working out the good things. He overcomes this financial giant for you in your life.

This is the primary foundation for the men of God's financial wealth. God tells us, check me here, if I don't open the windows of the sky and give you a blessing, you will have not enough room to obtain it.

The Bible specifically tells us that we deceive Him when we don't tithe. How do you cut off your feeding hand? That is exactly what we do when we refuse to tithe. God cannot continue to help us with finances unless he can trust us now with what we have.

Tithing is also a way to honor and thank God for what he gave us. He blessed you, and there's no better way to thank him than to give him what he gave you. It's an act of obedience and self-discipline.

He tells us explicitly that the first fruits of our development are his. Ten percent of what we get will belong to him. He commands us to ensure that food is in his house. It's a simple indication when we follow God that he is your first priority.

When we tithe, God asks us to test him, if he doesn't reproach him for us. He makes sure there's healthy fruit, whatever we do. The employers and corporate partners pay us on time. We are valued in our work and in our firms.

When we tithe, we live our financial lives according to the representatives of the Kingdom of God. It doesn't matter, therefore, what happens around you. You cannot be influenced by the rising global economy and inflation. What if the world could not afford to bring bread on his tables and cannot afford to help establish his kingdom? There is a reason this principle is in place for the faithful.

Within today's culture, many have forgotten the sense of having to tithe and make our daily offerings to Christ. People struggle financially and it does not seem to make good financial sense to have to pay any of our earnings.

We just have to look at it from a different perspective. With any donation, we need to give because we want to pay our taxes and not simply out of duty. Christians owe nothing to God, and if we think we can buy our own stairs to the capital, we're in for a huge surprise.

The tithe and sacrifices will be an act of obedience, and only a small portion of that for which God has blessed us is returned. All things exist because of the grace of God, and therefore, in fact, we only hold the riches we have as stewards for God's sake.

Essentially, since we are His servants and faithful, and have chosen not to tithe, we directly steal from ourselves.

<u>CONCLUSION</u>

The custom of tithing is generally connected to spiritual traditions and thus causes some controversy. Various spiritual denominations debate whether or not we will pay tithes based on their scriptural interpretation.

The tithe is often viewed as one of the peculiarities of sects such as Mormonism, or New Age doctrine.

When we pay an honest tithe, God promises to "open the gates of the city to you and to reward you, lest there be space for it." (Malachi 3:10).

Besides this reference, I shall strive to keep religion out of this discussion and concentrate on the theory and how it relates to the application of the Law of Attraction, and why and how it would function for you .

Paying tithing is an indication of a mental surplus as opposed to worrying about scarcity (Scare City!). It is an outward symbol of your trust and conviction that your needs can be met by the universe.

That may be especially poignant in these extraordinary times and a declaration that you are sure that the credit crunch will survive!

The word "Tithe" comes from the old English word "one-tenth," and the term "Tithe" normally refers to one-tenth of the rise or income, typically measured from the gross sum.

Usually you pay where you feel nearest to the source. This can be for a good cause or an agency that altruistically supports people or the environment. Usually the source of your spiritual advice is compensated, for example a church, synagogue or spiritual teacher.

It is better to pay as you earn-when the money arrives, figure out the tithe and pay it immediately. Alternatively, you slip down.

I myself treat it as a financial obligation just like payment of rent or a mortgage, because mentally I prefer to interpret it – rental of all the resources I and my family have made!

If you don't believe the spiritual side of it, then it could make you do something you haven't done before – budget! If you spend 10 percent of your income for a spiritual cause or a church, you must first account for the funds you get through in order to find out how much you will spend.

Only a careful attitude and interaction with money should foster long-term prosperity.

With regard to the law of attraction, the universe says that you have a lot to offer and are willing to give, that means you are open to receive more.

Tithing is an acknowledgment that we are both interconnected and interdependent. You cannot create any wealth by your own efforts alone. Only a painting or sculpture artist needs the raw materials, and the author needs pen and paper. Tithing recognizes the sacrifices made by others to your performance.

You know that, at the end of the day, you're not the center of money. You're in the middle. If you let some of the riches pass you and on, you must ensure that you remain in the flow.

Tithing is also a check on your money behavior.

Are you gullible, egotistic and self-centered?

I do not say if you don't pay tithing you are all those things, but it's definitely very difficult to have a negative attitude about money if you pay tithing at the same time. You will acquire it and share it without desiring or adoring it.

However, the payment of tithing does not function as an ATM.

It is about our spiritual relationship with money and the world, and it may be complicated to have these relations. Tithing cannot be used as a tool for "driving" any material reward out of God or the world. Tithing should be offered in a thankful and open heart.

We are truly happy and in our element when we give freely and try to make the lives of other people easier. We also benefit from paying tithing in this way.

If your company is stagnant and you don't tithe, it may be an idea to add this part of the flow to your donation and receipt.

Just DO and see how this great and powerful principle works for you. Thank you, Rich Love and Blessings, Rev. Dane Marks.